James Russell Lowell

Literary essays

Vol. 6

James Russell Lowell

Literary essays
Vol. 6

ISBN/EAN: 9783337810238

Printed in Europe, USA, Canada, Australia, Japan

Cover: Foto ©ninafisch / pixelio.de

More available books at **www.hansebooks.com**

LITERARY AND POLITICAL
ADDRESSES

BY

JAMES RUSSELL LOWELL

BOSTON AND NEW YORK
HOUGHTON, MIFFLIN AND COMPANY
The Riverside Press, Cambridge
M DCCC XCII

The Riverside Press, Cambridge, Mass., U. S. A.
Electrotyped and Printed by H. O. Houghton & Company.

CONTENTS

LITERARY AND POLITICAL AD-DRESSES

DEMOCRACY

INAUGURAL ADDRESS ON ASSUMING THE PRESIDENCY
OF THE BIRMINGHAM AND MIDLAND INSTITUTE,
BIRMINGHAM, ENGLAND, 6 OCTOBER, 1884.

HE must be a born leader or misleader of men,
or must have been sent into the world unfurnished
with that modulating and restraining balance-wheel
which we call a sense of humor, who, in old age,
has as strong a confidence in his opinions and in
the necessity of bringing the universe into conform-
ity with them as he had in youth. In a world
the very condition of whose being is that it should
be in perpetual flux, where all seems mirage, and
the one abiding thing is the effort to distinguish
realities from appearances, the elderly man must
be indeed of a singularly tough and valid fibre
who is certain that he has any clarified residuum of
experience, any assured verdict of reflection, that
deserves to be called an opinion, or who, even if
he had, feels that he is justified in holding mankind by the button while he is expounding it.
And in a world of daily — nay, almost hourly —

journalism, where every clever man, every man who thinks himself clever, or whom anybody else thinks clever, is called upon to deliver his judgment point-blank and at the word of command on every conceivable subject of human thought, or, on what sometimes seems to him very much the same thing, on every inconceivable display of human want of thought, there is such a spendthrift waste of all those commonplaces which furnish the permitted staple of public discourse that there is little chance of beguiling a new tune out of the one-stringed instrument on which we have been thrumming so long. In this desperate necessity one is often tempted to think that, if all the words of the dictionary were tumbled down in a heap and then all those fortuitous juxtapositions and combinations that made tolerable sense were picked out and pieced together, we might find among them some poignant suggestions towards novelty of thought or expression. But, alas! it is only the great poets who seem to have this unsolicited profusion of unexpected and incalculable phrase, this infinite variety of topic. For everybody else everything has been said before, and said over again after. He who has read his Aristotle will be apt to think that observation has on most points of general applicability said its last word, and he who has mounted the tower of Plato to look abroad from it will never hope to climb another with so lofty a vantage of speculation. Where it is so simple if not so easy a thing to hold one's peace, why add to the general confusion of tongues?

There is something disheartening, too, in being expected to fill up not less than a certain measure of time, as if the mind were an hour-glass, that need only be shaken and set on one end or the other, as the case may be, to run its allotted sixty minutes with decorous exactitude. I recollect being once told by the late eminent naturalist, Agassiz, that when he was to deliver his first lecture as professor (at Zürich, I believe) he had grave doubts of his ability to occupy the prescribed three quarters of an hour. He was speaking without notes, and glancing anxiously from time to time at the watch that lay before him on the desk. " When I had spoken a half hour," he said, " I had told them everything I knew in the world, everything! Then I began to repeat myself," he added, roguishly, "and I have done nothing else ever since." Beneath the humorous exaggeration of the story I seemed to see the face of a very serious and improving moral. And yet if one were to say only what he had to say and then stopped, his audience would feel defrauded of their honest measure. Let us take courage by the example of the French, whose exportation of Bordeaux wines increases as the area of their land in vineyards is diminished.

To me, somewhat hopelessly revolving these things, the undelayable year has rolled round, and I find myself called upon to say something in this place, where so many wiser men have spoken before me. Precluded, in my quality of national guest, by motives of taste and discretion, from dealing with any question of immediate and domestic concern, it seemed to me wisest, or at any rate most prudent, to choose a topic of comparatively abstract interest, and to ask your indulgence for a few somewhat generalized remarks on a matter concerning which I had some experimental knowledge, derived from the use of such eyes and ears as Nature had been pleased to endow me withal, and such report as I had been able to win from them. The subject which most readily suggested itself was the spirit and the working of those conceptions of life and polity which are lumped together, whether for reproach or commendation, under the name of Democracy. By temperament and education of a conservative turn, I saw the last years of that quaint Arcadia which French travellers saw with delighted amazement a century ago, and have watched the change (to me a sad one) from an agricultural to a proletary population. The testimony of Balaam should carry some conviction. I have grown to manhood and am now growing old with the growth of this system of government in my native land, have watched its advances, or what some would call its encroachments, gradual and irresistible as those of a glacier, have been an earwitness to the forebodings of wise and good and timid men, and have lived to see those forebodings belied by the course of events, which is apt to show itself humorously careless of the reputation of prophets. I recollect hearing a sagacious old gentleman say in 1840 that the doing away with the property qualification for suffrage twenty years before had been the ruin of the State of Massachusetts; that it had put public credit and private estate alike at the mercy of demagogues. I lived to see that Commonwealth twenty odd years later paying the interest on her bonds in gold, though it cost her sometimes nearly three for one to keep her faith, and that while suffering an unparalleled drain of men and treasure in helping to sustain the unity and self-respect of the nation.

If universal suffrage has worked ill in our larger cities, as it certainly has, this has been mainly because the hands that wielded it were untrained to its use. There the election of a majority of the trustees of the public money is controlled by the most ignorant and vicious of a population which has come to us from abroad, wholly unpractised in self-government and incapable of assimilation by American habits and methods. But the finances of our towns, where the native tradition is still dominant and whose affairs are discussed and settled in a public assembly of the people, have been in general honestly and prudently administered. Even in manufacturing towns, where a majority of the voters live by their daily wages, it is not so often the recklessness as the moderation of public expenditure that surprises an old-fashioned observer. "The beggar is in the saddle at last," cries Proverbial Wisdom. "Why, in the name of all former experience, does n't he ride to the Devil?" Because in the very act of mounting he ceased to be a beggar and became part owner of the piece of property he bestrides. The last thing we need be anxious about is property. It always has friends

or the means of making them. If riches have wings
to fly away from their owner, they have wings also
to escape danger.

I hear America sometimes playfully accused of
sending you all your storms, and am in the habit
of parrying the charge by alleging that we are enabled to do this because, in virtue of our protective
system, we can afford to make better bad weather
than anybody else. And what wiser use could we
make of it than to export it in return for the paupers which some European countries are good
enough to send over to us who have not attained
to the same skill in the manufacture of them?
But bad weather is not the worst thing that is laid
at our door. A French gentleman, not long ago,
forgetting Burke's monition of how unwise it is to
draw an indictment against a whole people, has
charged us with the responsibility of whatever he
finds disagreeable in the morals or manners of his
countrymen. If M. Zola or some other competent
witness would only go into the box and tell us what
those morals and manners were before our example
corrupted them! But I confess that I find little
to interest and less to edify me in these international bandyings of " You 're another."

I shall address myself to a single point only in
the long list of offences of which we are more or
less gravely accused, because that really includes
all the rest. It is that we are infecting the Old
World with what seems to be thought the entirely
new disease of Democracy. It is generally people
who are in what are called easy circumstances who

can afford the leisure to treat themselves to a handsome complaint, and these experience an immediate alleviation when once they have found a sonorous Greek name to abuse it by. There is something consolatory also, something flattering to their sense of personal dignity, and to that conceit of singularity which is the natural recoil from our uneasy consciousness of being commonplace, in thinking ourselves victims of a malady by which no one had ever suffered before. Accordingly they find it simpler to class under one comprehensive heading whatever they find offensive to their nerves, their tastes, their interests, or what they suppose to be their opinions, and christen it Democracy, much as physicians label every obscure disease gout, or as cross-grained fellows lay their ill-temper to the weather. But is it really a new ailment, and, if it be, is America answerable for it? Even if she were, would it account for the phylloxera, and hoof-and-mouth disease, and bad harvests, and bad English, and the German bands, and the Boers, and all the other discomforts with which these later days have vexed the souls of them that go in chariots? Yet I have seen the evil example of Democracy in America cited as the source and origin of things quite as heterogeneous and quite as little connected with it by any sequence of cause and effect. Surely this ferment is nothing new. It has been at work for centuries, and we are more conscious of it only because in this age of publicity, where the newspapers offer a rostrum to whoever has a grievance, or fancies that he has, the bubbles

and scum thrown up by it are more noticeable on
the surface than in those dumb ages when there
was a cover of silence and suppression on the caul-
dron.   Bernardo Navagero, speaking of the Prov-
inces of Lower Austria in 1546, tells us that " in
them there are five sorts of persons, Clergy, Barons, Nobles, Burghers, and Peasants. Of these last
no account is made, *because they have no voice in
the Diet.*" [1]

Nor was it among the people that subversive or
mistaken doctrines had their rise. A Father of the
Church said that property was theft many centuries before Proudhon was born.   Bourdaloue re-
affirmed it.   Montesquieu was the inventor of national workshops, and of the theory that the State
owed every man a living. Nay, was not the Church
herself the first organized Democracy? A few
centuries ago the chief end of man was to keep
his soul alive, and then the little kernel of leaven
that sets the gases at work was religious, and produced the Reformation.   Even in that, far-sighted
persons like the Emperor Charles V. saw the germ
of political and social revolution. Now that the
chief end of man seems to have become the keeping of the body alive, and as comfortably alive as

---

[1] Below the Peasants, it should be remembered, was still another even more helpless class, the servile farm-laborers. The
same witness informs us that of the extraordinary imposts the
Peasants paid nearly twice as much in proportion to their estimated property as the Barons, Nobles, and Burghers together.
Moreover, the upper classes were assessed at their own valuation,
while they arbitrarily fixed that of the Peasants, who had no
voice. (*Relazioni degli Ambasciatori Veneti*, Serie I., tomo i , pp.
378, 379, 389.)

possible, the leaven also has become wholly political and social. But there had also been social upheavals before the Reformation and contemporaneously with it, especially among men of Teutonic race. The Reformation gave outlet and direction to an unrest already existing. Formerly the immense majority of men — our brothers — knew only their sufferings, their wants, and their desirès. They are beginning now to know their opportunity and their power. All persons who see deeper than their plates are rather inclined to thank God for it than to bewail it, for the sores of Lazarus have a poison in them against which Dives has no antidote.

There can be no doubt that the spectacle of a great and prosperous Democracy on the other side of the Atlantic must react powerfully on the aspirations and political theories of men in the Old World who do not find things to their mind ; but, whether for good or evil, it should not be overlooked that the acorn from which it sprang was ripened on the British oak. Every successive swarm that has gone out from this *officina gentium* has, when left to its own instincts — may I not call them hereditary instincts ? — assumed a more or less thoroughly democratic form. This would seem to show, what I believe to be the fact, that the British Constitution, under whatever disguises of prudence or decorum, is essentially democratic. England, indeed, may be called a monarchy with democratic tendencies, the United States a democracy with conservative instincts. People are continually saying that America is in the air, and I am glad to think it is, since this means only that a clearer conception of human claims and human duties is beginning to be prevalent. The discontent with the existing order of things, however, pervaded the atmosphere wherever the conditions were favorable, long before Columbus, seeking the back door of Asia, found himself knocking at the front door of America. I say wherever the conditions were favorable, for it is certain that the germs of disease do not stick or find a prosperous field for their development and noxious activity unless where the simplest sanitary precautions have been neglected. "For this effect defective comes by cause," as Polonius said long ago. It is only by instigation of the wrongs of men that what are called the Rights of Man become turbulent and dangerous. It is then only that they syllogize unwelcome truths. It is not the insurrections of ignorance that are dangerous, but the revolts of intelligence : —

> " The wicked and the weak rebel in vain,
> Slaves by their own compulsion."

Had the governing classes in France during the last century paid as much heed to their proper business as to their pleasures or manners, the guillotine need never have severed that spinal marrow of orderly and secular tradition through which in a normally constituted state the brain sympathizes with the extremities and sends will and impulsion thither. It is only when the reasonable and practicable are denied that men demand the unreasonable and impracticable ; only when the possible is made difficult that they fancy the impossible to be easy. Fairy tales are made out of the dreams of the poor. No; the sentiment which lies at the root of democracy is nothing new. I am speaking always of a sentiment, a spirit, and not of a form of government; for this was but the outgrowth of the other and not its cause. This sentiment is merely an expression of the natural wish of people to have a hand, if need be a controlling hand, in the management of their own affairs. What is new is that they are more and more gaining that control, and learning more and more how to be worthy of it. What we used to call the tendency or drift — what we are being taught to call more wisely the evolution of things — has for some time been setting steadily in this direction. There is no good in arguing with the inevitable. The only argument available with an east wind is to put on your overcoat. And in this case, also, the prudent will prepare themselves to encounter what they cannot prevent. Some people advise us to put on the brakes, as if the movement of which we are conscious were that of a railway train running down an incline. But a metaphor is no argument, though it be sometimes the gunpowder to drive one home and imbed it in the memory. Our disquiet comes of what nurses and other experienced persons call growing-pains, and need not seriously alarm us. They are what every generation before us — certainly every generation since the invention of printing — has gone through with more or less good fortune. To the door of every generation there comes a knocking, and unless the household, like the Thane of Cawdor and his wife, have been doing some deed without a name, they need not shudder. It turns out at worst to be a poor relation who wishes to come in out of the cold. The porter always grumbles and is slow to open. "Who's there, in the name of Beelzebub?" he mutters. Not a change for the better in our human housekeeping has ever taken place that wise and good men have not opposed it, — have not prophesied with the alderman that the world would wake up to find its throat cut in consequence of it. The world, on the contrary, wakes up, rubs its eyes, yawns, stretches itself, and goes about its business as if nothing had happened. Suppression of the slave trade, abolition of slavery, trade unions, — at all of these excellent people shook their heads despondingly, and murmured "Ichabod." But the trade unions are now debating instead of conspiring, and we all read their discussions with comfort and hope, sure that they are learning the business of citizenship and the difficulties of practical legislation.

One of the most curious of these frenzies of exclusion was that against the emancipation of the Jews. All share in the government of the world was denied for centuries to perhaps the ablest, certainly the most tenacious, race that had ever lived in it — the race to whom we owed our religion and the purest spiritual stimulus and consolation to be found in all literature — a race in which ability seems as natural and hereditary as the curve of their noses, and whose blood, furtively mingling with the bluest bloods in Europe, has quickened them with its own indomitable impulsion. We drove them into a corner, but they had their revenge, as the wronged are always sure to have it sooner or later. They made their corner the counter and banking-house of the world, and thence they rule it and us with the ignobler sceptre of finance. Your grandfathers mobbed Priestley only that you might set up his statue and make Birmingham the headquarters of English Unitarianism. We hear it said sometimes that this is an age of transition, as if that made matters clearer ; but can any one point us to an age that was not ? If he could, he would show us an age of stagnation. The question for us, as it has been for all before us, is to make the transition gradual and easy, to see that our points are right so that the train may not come to grief. For we should remember that nothing is more natural for people whose education has been neglected than to spell evolution with an initial " r." A great man struggling with the storms of fate has been called a sublime spectacle ; but surely a great man wrestling with these new forces that have come into the world, mastering them and controlling them to beneficent ends, would be a yet sublimer. Here is not a danger, and if there were it would be only a better school of manhood, a nobler scope for ambition. I have hinted that what people are afraid of in democracy is less the thing itself than what they conceive to be its necessary adjuncts and consequences. It is supposed to reduce all mankind to a dead level of mediocrity in character and culture, to vulgarize men's conceptions of life, and therefore their code of morals, manners, and conduct — to endanger the rights of property and possession. But I believe that the real gravamen of the charges lies in the habit it has of making itself generally disagreeable by asking the Powers that Be at the most inconvenient moment whether they are the powers that ought to be. If the powers that be are in a condition to give a satisfactory answer to this inevitable question, they need feel in no way discomfited by it.

Few people take the trouble of trying to find out what democracy really is. Yet this would be a great help, for it is our lawless and uncertain thoughts, it is the indefiniteness of our impressions, that fill darkness, whether mental or physical, with spectres and hobgoblins. Democracy is nothing more than an experiment in government, more likely to succeed in a new soil, but likely to be tried in all soils, which must stand or fall on its own merits as others have done before it. For there is no trick of perpetual motion in politics any more than in mechanics. President Lincoln defined democracy to be " the government of the people by the people for the people." This is a sufficiently compact statement of it as a political arrangement. Theodore Parker said that " Democracy meant not ' I 'm as good as you are,' but ' You 're as good as I am.' " And this is the ethical conception of it, necessary as a complement of the other; a conception which, could it be made actual and practical,

would easily solve all the riddles that the old
sphinx of political and social economy who sits by
the roadside has been proposing to mankind from
the beginning, and which mankind have shown such
a singular talent for answering wrongly. In this
sense Christ was the first true democrat that ever
breathed, as the old dramatist Dekker said he was
the first true gentleman. The characters may be
easily doubled, so strong is the likeness between
them. A beautiful and profound parable of the
Persian poet Jellaladeen tells us that " One knocked
at the Beloved's door, and a voice asked from
within ' Who is there?' and he answered ' It is I.'
Then the voice said, ' This house will not hold me
and thee;' and the door was not opened. Then
went the lover into the desert and fasted and prayed
in solitude, and after a year he returned and
knocked again at the door ; and again the voice
asked ' Who is there?' and he said ' It is thyself ;'
and the door was opened to him." But that is
idealism, you will say, and this is an only too practical world. I grant it ; but I am one of those who
believe that the real will never find an irremova-
ble basis till it rests on the ideal. It used to be
thought that a democracy was possible only in a
small territory, and this is doubtless true of a democracy strictly defined, for in such all the citizens
decide directly upon every question of public concern in a general assembly. An example still survives in the tiny Swiss canton of Appenzell. But
this immediate intervention of the people in their
own affairs is not of the essence of democracy; it

is not necessary, nor indeed, in most cases, practicable. Democracies to which Mr. Lincoln's definition would fairly enough apply have existed, and now exist, in which, though the supreme authority reside in the people, yet they can act only indirectly on the national policy. This generation has seen a democracy with an imperial figurehead, and in all that have ever existed the body politic has never embraced all the inhabitants included within its territory, the right to share in the direction of affairs has been confined to citizens, and citizenship has been further restricted by various limitations, sometimes of property, sometimes of nativity, and always of age and sex.

The framers of the American Constitution were far from wishing or intending to found a democracy in the strict sense of the word, though, as was inevitable, every expansion of the scheme of government they elaborated has been in a democratical direction. But this has been generally the slow result of growth, and not the sudden innovation of theory; in fact, they had a profound disbelief in theory, and knew better than to commit the folly of breaking with the past. They were not seduced by the French fallacy that a new system of government could be ordered like a new suit of clothes. They would as soon have thought of ordering a new suit of flesh and skin. It is only on the roaring loom of time that the stuff is woven for such a vesture of their thought and experience as they were meditating. They recognized fully the value of tradition and habit as the great allies of perma-

nence and stability. They all had that distaste for
innovation which belonged to their race, and many
of them a distrust of human nature derived from
their creed. The day of sentiment was over, and
no dithyrambic affirmations or fine-drawn analyses
of the Rights of Man would serve their present
turn. This was a practical question, and they addressed themselves to it as men of knowledge and
judgment should. Their problem was how to adapt
English principles and precedents to the new conditions of American life, and they solved it with
singular discretion. They put as many obstacles
as they could contrive, not in the way of the people's will, but of their whim. With few exceptions
they probably admitted the logic of the then accepted syllogism, — democracy, anarchy, despotism.
But this formula was framed upon the experience
of small cities shut up to stew within their narrow
walls, where the number of citizens made but an
inconsiderable fraction of the inhabitants, where
every passion was reverberated from house to
house and from man to man with gathering rumor
till every impulse became gregarious and therefore
inconsiderate, and every popular assembly needed
but an infusion of eloquent sophistry to turn it
into a mob, all the more dangerous because sancti-
fied with the formality of law.[1]

Fortunately their case was wholly different.

[1] The effect of the electric telegraph in reproducing this troop-
ing of emotion and perhaps of opinion is yet to be measured. The
effect of Darwinism as a disintegrator of humanitarianism is also
to be reckoned with.

They were to legislate for a widely scattered population and for States already practised in the discipline of a partial independence. They had an unequalled opportunity and enormous advantages. The material they had to work upon was already democratical by instinct and habitude. It was tempered to their hands by more than a century's schooling in self-government. They had but to give permanent and conservative form to a ductile mass. In giving impulse and direction to their new institutions, especially in supplying them with checks and balances, they had a great help and safeguard in their federal organization. The different, sometimes conflicting, interests and social systems of the several States made existence as a Union and coalescence into a nation conditional on a constant practice of moderation and compromise. The very elements of disintegration were the best guides in political training. Their children learned the lesson of compromise only too well, and it was the application of it to a question of fundamental morals that cost us our civil war. We learned once for all that compromise makes a good umbrella but a poor roof; that it is a temporary expedient, often wise in party politics, almost sure to be unwise in statesmanship.

Has not the trial of democracy in America proved, on the whole, successful? If it had not, would the Old World be vexed with any fears of its proving contagious? This trial would have been less severe could it have been made with a people homogeneous in race, language, and traditions, whereas the United States have been called on to absorb and assimilate enormous, masses of foreign population, heterogeneous in all these respects, and drawn mainly from that class which might fairly say that the world was not their friend, nor the world's law. The previous condition too often justified the traditional Irishman, who, landing in New York and asked what his politics were, inquired if there was a Government there, and on being told that there was, retorted, "Thin I'm agin it!" We have taken from Europe the poorest, the most ignorant, the most turbulent of her people, and have made them over into good citizens, who have added to our wealth, and who are ready to die in defence of a country and of institutions which they know to be worth dying for. The exceptions have been (and they are lamentable exceptions) where these hordes of ignorance and poverty have coagulated in great cities. But the social system is yet to seek which has not to look the same terrible wolf in the eyes. On the other hand, at this very moment Irish peasants are buying up the worn-out farms of Massachusetts, and making them productive again by the same virtues of industry and thrift that once made them profitable to the English ancestors of the men who are deserting them. To have achieved even these prosaic results (if you choose to call them so), and that out of materials the most discordant, — I might say the most recalcitrant, — argues a certain beneficent virtue in the system that could do it, and is not to be accounted for by mere luck. Carlyle said scornfully that America meant only roast turkey every day for everybody. He forgot that States, as Bacon said of wars, go on their bellies. As for the security of property, it should be tolerably well secured in a country where every other man hopes to be rich, even though the only property qualification be the ownership of two hands that add to the general wealth. Is it not the best security for anything to interest the largest possible number of persons in its preservation and the smallest in its division? In point of fact, far-seeing men count the increasing power of wealth and its combinations as one of the chief dangers with which the institutions of the United States are threatened in the not distant future. The right of individual property is no doubt the very corner-stone of civilization as hitherto understood, but I am a little impatient of being told that property is entitled to exceptional consideration because it bears all the burdens of the State. It bears those, indeed, which can most easily be borne, but poverty pays with its person the chief expenses of war, pestilence, and famine. Wealth should not forget this, for poverty is beginning to think of it now and then. Let me not be misunderstood. I see as clearly as any man possibly can, and rate as highly, the value of wealth, and of hereditary wealth, as the security of refinement, the feeder of all those arts that ennoble and beautify life, and as making a country worth living in. Many an ancestral hall here in England has been a nursery of that culture which has been of example and benefit to all. Old gold has a civilizing virtue which new gold must grow old to be capable of secreting.

I should not think of coming before you to defend or to criticise any form of government. All have their virtues, all their defects, and all have illustrated one period or another in the history of the race, with signal services to humanity and culture. There is not one that could stand a cynical cross-examination by an experienced criminal lawyer, except that of a perfectly wise and perfectly good despot, such as the world has never seen, except in that white-haired king of Browning's, who

> " Lived long ago
> In the morning of the world,
> When Earth was nearer Heaven than now."

The English race, if they did not invent government by discussion, have at least carried it nearest to perfection in practice. It seems a very safe and reasonable contrivance for occupying the attention of the country, and is certainly a better way of settling questions than by push of pike. Yet, if one should ask it why it should not rather be called government by gabble, it would have to fumble in its pocket a good while before it found the change for a convincing reply. As matters stand, too, it is beginning to be doubtful whether Parliament and Congress sit at Westminster and Washington or in the editors' rooms of the leading journals, so thoroughly is everything debated before the authorized and responsible debaters get on their legs. And what shall we say of government by a majority of voices? To a person who in the last century

would have called himself an Impartial Observer,
a numerical preponderance seems, on the whole, as
clumsy a way of arriving at truth as could well be
devised, but experience has apparently shown it
to be a convenient arrangement for determining
what may be expedient or advisable or practicable
at any given moment. Truth, after all, wears a
different face to everybody, and it would be too
tedious to wait till all were agreed. She is said to
lie at the bottom of a well, for the very reason,
perhaps, that whoever looks down in search of her
sees his own image at the bottom, and is persuaded
not only that he has seen the goddess, but that she
is far better-looking than he had imagined.

The arguments against universal suffrage are
equally unanswerable. "What," we exclaim,
"shall Tom, Dick, and Harry have as much weight
in the scale as I?" Of course, nothing could be
more absurd. And yet universal suffrage has not
been the instrument of greater unwisdom than contrivances of a more select description. Assemblies
could be mentioned composed entirely of Masters
of Arts and Doctors in Divinity which have sometimes shown traces of human passion or prejudice
in their votes. Have the Serene Highnesses and
Enlightened Classes carried on the business of
Mankind so well, then, that there is no use in trying a less costly method? The democratic theory
is that those Constitutions are likely to prove stead-
iest which have the broadest base, that the right to
vote makes a safety-valve of every voter, and that
the best way of teaching a man how to vote is to

give him the chance of practice. For the question is no longer the academic one, " Is it wise to give every man the ballot? " but rather the practical one, " Is it prudent to deprive whole classes of it any longer? " It may be conjectured that it is cheaper in the long run to lift men up than to hold them down, and that the ballot in their hands is less dangerous to society than a sense of wrong in their heads. At any rate this is the dilemma to which the drift of opinion has been for some time sweeping us, and in politics a dilemma is a more unmanageable thing to hold by the horns than a wolf by the ears. It is said that the right of suffrage is not valued when it is indiscriminately bestowed, and there may be some truth in this, for I have observed that what men prize most is a privilege, even if it be that of chief mourner at a funeral. But is there not danger that it will be valued at more than its worth if denied, and that some illegitimate way will be sought to make up for the want of it? Men who have a voice in public affairs are at once affiliated with one or other of the great parties between which society is divided, merge their individual hopes and opinions in its safer, because more generalized, hopes and opinions, are disciplined by its tactics, and acquire, to a certain degree, the orderly qualities of an army. They no longer belong to a class, but to a body corporate. Of one thing, at least, we may be certain, that, under whatever method of helping things to go wrong man's wit can contrive, those who have the divine right to govern will be found to govern in the end, and that the highest privilege to which the majority of mankind can aspire is that of being governed by those wiser than they.   Universal suffrage has in the United States sometimes been made the instrument of inconsiderate changes, under the notion of reform, and this from a misconception of the true meaning of popular government.   One of these has been the substitution in many of the States of popular election for official selection in the choice of judges.   The same system applied to military officers was the source of much evil during our civil war, and, I believe, had to be abandoned.   But it has been also true that on all great questions of national policy a reserve of prudence and discretion has been brought out at the critical moment to turn the scale in favor of a wiser decision.   An appeal to the reason of the people has never been known to fail in the long run.   It is, perhaps, true that, by effacing the principle of passive obedience, democracy, ill understood, has slackened the spring of that ductility to discipline which is essential to " the unity and married calm of States."   But I feel assured that experience and necessity will cure this evil, as they have shown their power to cure others.   And under what frame of policy have evils ever been remedied till they became intolerable, and shook men out of their indolent indifference through their fears?

We are told that the inevitable result of democracy is to sap the foundations of personal independence, to weaken the principle of authority, to lessen the respect due to eminence, whether in station, virtue, or genius. If these things were so, society could not hold together. Perhaps the best forcing-house of robust individuality would be where public opinion is inclined to be most over-bearing, as he must be of heroic temper who should walk along Piccadilly at the height of the season in a soft hat. As for authority, it is one of the symptoms of the time that the religious reverence for it is declining everywhere, but this is due partly to the fact that state-craft is no longer looked upon as a mystery, but as a business, and partly to the decay of superstition, by which I mean the habit of respecting what we are told to respect rather than what is respectable in itself. There is more rough and tumble in the American democracy than is altogether agreeable to people of sensitive nerves and refined habits, and the people take their politi-cal duties lightly and laughingly, as is, perhaps, neither unnatural nor unbecoming in a young giant. Democracies can no more jump away from their own shadows than the rest of us can. They no doubt sometimes make mistakes and pay honor to men who do not deserve it. But they do this because they believe them worthy of it, and though it be true that the idol is the measure of the wor-shipper, yet the worship has in it the germ of a no-bler religion. But is it democracies alone that fall into these errors? I, who have seen it proposed to erect a statue to Hudson, the railway king, and have heard Louis Napoleon hailed as the saviour of society by men who certainly had no democratic associations or leanings, am not ready to think so.

But democracies have likewise their finer instincts. I have also seen the wisest statesman and most pregnant speaker of our generation, a man of humble birth and ungainly manners, of little culture beyond what his own genius supplied, become more absolute in power than any monarch of modern times through the reverence of his countrymen for his honesty, his wisdom, his sincerity, his faith in God and man, and the nobly humane simplicity of his character. And I remember another whom popular respect enveloped as with a halo, the least vulgar of men, the most austerely genial, and the most independent of opinion. Wherever he went he never met a stranger, but everywhere neighbors and friends proud of him as their ornament and decoration. Institutions which could bear and breed such men as Lincoln and Emerson had surely some energy for good. No, amid all the fruitless turmoil and miscarriage of the world, if there be one thing steadfast and of favorable omen, one thing to make optimism distrust its own obscure distrust, it is the rooted instinct in men to admire what is better and more beautiful than themselves. The touchstone of political and social institutions is their ability to supply them with worthy objects of this sentiment, which is the very tap-root of civilization and progress. There would seem to be no readier way of feeding it with the elements of growth and vigor than such an organization of society as will enable men to respect themselves, and so to justify them in respecting others.

Such a result is quite possible under other conditions than those of an avowedly democratical Constitution. For I take it that the real essence of democracy was fairly enough defined by the, First Napoleon when he said that the French Revolution meant "la carrière ouverte aux ta-lents" — a clear pathway for merit of whatever kind. I should be inclined to paraphrase this by calling democracy that form of society, no matter what its political classification, in which every man had a chance and knew that he had it. If a man can climb, and feels himself encouraged to climb, from a coalpit to the highest position for which he is fitted, he can well afford to be indifferent what name is given to the government under which he lives. The Bailli of Mirabeau, uncle of the more famous tribune of that name, wrote in 1771: "The English are, in my opinion, a hundred times more agitated and more unfortunate than the very Algerines themselves, because they do not know and will not know till the destruction of their over-swollen power, which I believe very near, whether they are monarchy, aristocracy, or democracy, and wish to play the part of all three." England has not been obliging enough to fulfil the Bailli's prophecy, and perhaps it was this very carelessness about the name, and concern about the substance of popular government, this skill in getting the best out of things as they are, in utilizing all the motives which influence men, and in giving one direction to many impulses, that has been a principal factor of her greatness and power. Perhaps it is fortu-

nate to have an unwritten Constitution, for men
are prone to be tinkering the work of their own
hands, whereas they are more willing to let time
and circumstance mend or modify what time and
circumstance have made. All free governments,
whatever their name, are in reality governments
by public opinion, and it is on the quality of this
public opinion that their prosperity depends. It
is, therefore, their first duty to purify the element
from which they draw the breath of life. With
the growth of democracy grows also the fear, if
not the danger, that this atmosphere may be corrupted with poisonous exhalations from lower and
more malarious levels, and the question of sanita-
tion becomes more instant and pressing. Democracy in its best sense is merely the letting in of
light and air. Lord Sherbrooke, with his usual
epigrammatic terseness, bids you educate your
future rulers. But would this alone be a sufficient
safeguard? To educate the intelligence is to enlarge the horizon of its desires and wants. And
it is well that this should be so. But the enterprise must go deeper and prepare the way for sat-
isfying those desires and wants in so far as they
are legitimate. What is really ominous of danger
to the existing order of things is not democracy
(which, properly understood, is a conservative
force), but the Socialism, which may find a ful-
crum in it. If we cannot equalize conditions and
fortunes any more than we can equalize the brains
of men — and a very sagacious person has said
that "where two men ride of a horse one must ride

behind " — we can yet, perhaps, do something to correct those methods and influences that lead to enormous inequalities, and to prevent their growing more enormous. It is all very well to pooh-pooh Mr. George and to prove him mistaken in his political economy. I do not believe that land should be divided because the quantity of it is limited by nature. Of what may this not be said? *A fortiori*, we might on the same principle insist on a division of human wit, for I have observed that the quantity of this has been even more inconveniently limited. Mr. George himself has an inequitably large share of it. But he is right in his impelling motive; right, also, I am convinced, in insisting that humanity makes a part, by far the most important part, of political economy; and in thinking man to be of more concern and more convincing than the longest columns of figures in the world. For unless you include human nature in your addition, your total is sure to be wrong and your deductions from it fallacious. Communism means barbarism, but Socialism means, or wishes to mean, coöperation and community of interests, sympathy, the giving to the hands not so large a share as to the brains, but a larger share than hitherto in the wealth they must combine to produce — means, in short, the practical application of Christianity to life, and has in it the secret of an orderly and benign reconstruction. State Socialism would cut off the very roots in personal character — self-help, forethought, and frugality — which nourish and sustain the trunk and branches of every vigorous Commonwealth.

I do not believe in violent changes, nor do I expect them. Things in possession have a very firm grip. One of the strongest cements of society is the conviction of mankind that the state of things into which they are born is a part of the order of the universe, as natural, let us say, as that the sun should go round the earth. It is a conviction that they will not surrender except on compulsion, and a wise society should look to it that this compulsion be not put upon them. For the individual man there is no radical cure, outside of human nature itself, for the evils to which human natvre is heir. The rule will always hold good that you must

"Be your own palace or the world 's your gaol."

But for artificial evils, for evils that spring from want of thought, thought must find a remedy somewhere. There has been no period of time in which wealth has been more sensible of its duties than now. It builds hospitals, it establishes missions among the poor, it endows schools. It is one of the advantages of accumulated wealth, and of the leisure it renders possible, that people have time to think of the wants and sorrows of their fellows. But all these remedies are partial and palliative merely. It is as if we should apply plasters to a single pustule of the small-pox with a view of driving out the disease. The true way is to discover and to extirpate the germs. As society is now constituted these are in the air it breathes, in the water it drinks, in things that seem, and which it has always believed, to be the most innocent and healthful. The evil elements it neglects corrupt these in their springs and pollute them in their courses. Let us be of good cheer, however, remembering that the misfortunes hardest to bear are those which never come. The world has outlived much, and will outlive a great deal more, and men have contrived to be happy in it. It has shown the strength of its constitution in nothing more than in surviving the quack medicines it has tried. In the scales of the destinies brawn will never weigh so much as brain. Our healing is not in the storm or in the whirlwind, it is not in monarchies, or aristocracies, or democracies, but will be revealed by the still small voice that speaks to the conscience and the heart, prompting us to a wider and wiser humanity.

GARFIELD

SPOKEN ON THE DEATH OF PRESIDENT GARFIELD AT THE
MEMORIAL MEETING IN EXETER HALL, LONDON, 24
SEPTEMBER, 1881.

INTRODUCTORY NOTE.[1]

ONE thing and one only makes the record of the meeting at Exeter Hall on the 24th September worthy of separate publication, and confers on it a certain distinction. Not what was said, but where it was said, in unison with what other voices, and in what atmosphere of sympathy, as spontaneous as it was universal, gives to the words spoken here their true point and emphasis. Never before have Americans, speaking in England, felt so clearly that they were in the land, not only of their fathers, but of their brethren,

"Their elder brothers, but one in blood."

For the first time their common English tongue found its true office when Mother and Daughter spoke comforting words to each other over a sorrow, which, if nearer to one, was shared by both. English blood, made up of the best drops from the veins of many conquering, organizing, and colonizing races, is a blood to be proud of, and most plainly vindicates its claim to dominion when it recognizes kinship through sympathy with what is simple, steadfast, and religious in character. When we

---

[1] Printed first as a preface to the memorial volume, containing a record of the proceedings at the Exeter Hall meeting.

learn to respect each other for the good qualities in each, we are helping to produce and foster them.

It is often said that sentimental motives never guide or modify the policy of nations, and it is no doubt true that state-craft more and more means business, and not sentiment; yet men as old as the late Lord Stratford de Redcliffe could remember at least two occasions during their lives when a sentiment, and that, too, a literary sentiment, had much to do with the shaping of events and the new birth of nations. We would not over-estimate the permanent value of this outburst of feeling on both sides the sea, of this grasp of the hand across a recent grave, but we may safely affirm that they were genuine, and had, therefore, something of the enduring virtue that belongs to what is genuine, and to that only. It is something that two great nations have looked at each other kindly through their tears. It will at least be more awkward to quarrel hereafter. The sight of the British flag at half-mast on the day of an American funeral was something to set men thinking, and that fruitfully, of the great duty that is laid upon the English race among mankind. Well may we be proud of the Ancient Mother, and we will see to it that she have no reason to be ashamed of her children.

It behoves us Americans who have experienced nothing but the kindness and hospitality and sympathy of England, to express thus publicly our sense of them. Especially would we thank the venerable prelate whose address we are permitted to include in this little volume. And emphatically would we express our conviction that the wreath sent with such touching delicacy of feeling by her Majesty the Queen to be laid upon the bier of President Garfield, will be hung upon a golden nail in the Temple of Concord.

LADIES AND GENTLEMEN, COUNTRYMEN AND
COUNTRYWOMEN: The object of this meeting, as
you all know, is to testify our respect for the character and services of the late President Garfield,
and in so doing to offer such consolation as is possible to a noble mother and a noble wife, suffering
as few women have been called upon to suffer.   It
may seem a paradox, but the only alleviation of
such grief is a sense of the greatness and costliness
of the sacrifice that gave birth to it, and this sense
is brought home to us by the measure in which
others appreciate our loss.   It is no exaggeration to
say that the recent profoundly touching spectacle
of womanly devotedness in its simplicity, its con-
stancy, and its dignity has moved the heart of
mankind in a manner without any precedent in
living memory.   But to Americans everywhere it
comes home with a pang of mingled sorrow, pride,
and unspeakable domestic tenderness that none
but ourselves can feel.   This pang is made more
poignant by exile, and yet you will all agree with
me in feeling that the universal sympathy expressed
here by all classes and conditions of men has made
us sensible as never before, that, if we are in a
strange, we are not in a foreign land, and that if
we are not at home we are at least in what Haw-
thorne so aptly called the Old Home.   I should
gladly dwell more at length upon this fact, so consoling and so full of all good omen, but I must not
infringe on the resolutions which will be presented
to you by others.   Yet I should do injustice to

your feelings, no less than to my own, if I did not offer here our grateful acknowledgments to the august lady who, herself not unacquainted with grief, has shown so repeatedly and so touchingly how true a woman's heart may beat under the royal purple.

On an occasion like this, when we are met together that we may give vent to a common feeling so deep and so earnest as to thrust aside every consideration of self, the wish of us all must be that what is said here should be simple, strong, and manly as the character of the illustrious magistrate so untimely snatched from us in the very seed-time of noble purpose, that would have sprung up in service as noble, — that we should be as tender and true as she has shown herself to be in whose bereavement we reverently claim to share as children of the blessed country that gave birth to him and to her. We cannot find words that could reach that lofty level. This is no place for the turnings and windings of dexterous rhetoric. In the presence of that death-scene so homely, so human, so august in its unostentatious heroism, the commonplaces of ordinary eulogy stammer with the sudden shame of their own ineptitude. Were we allowed to follow the natural promptings of our hearts, we would sum up all praise in the sacred old words, "Well done, thou good and faithful servant."

That death-scene was more than singular; it was unexampled. The whole civilized world was gathered about it in the breathless suspense of anxious solicitude, listened to the difficult breathing, counted the fluttering pulse, was cheered by the momentary rally and saddened by the inevitable relapse. And let us thank God and take courage when we reflect that it was through the manliness, the patience, the religious fortitude of the splendid victim that the tie of human brotherhood was thrilled to a consciousness of its sacred function. The one touch of nature that makes the whole world kin is a touch of heroism, our sympathy with which dignifies and ennobles. Science has wrought no greater marvel in the service of humanity than when it gave the world a common nervous system, and thus made mankind capable of a simultaneous emotion.

One remarkable feature of that death-scene was the imperturbable good nature of the sufferer. This has been sometimes called a peculiarly American quality, — a weakness if in excess or misapplied, but beautiful in its own genial place, as there and then it was. General Garfield once said to a friend, " They tell me it is a defect of my character, but I cannot hate anybody." Like Socrates, he seemed good-humored even with death, though there have been few men from whom death has ever wrenched a fairer heritage of opportunity. Physicians tell us that all men die well, but surely he was no ordinary man who could die well daily for eleven agonizing weeks, and of whom it could be said at last, —

> " He nothing common did, or mean,
> Upon that memorable scene."

A fibre capable of such strain and wear as that is

used only in the making of heroic natures. Twenty
years ago General Garfield offered his life to his
country, and he has died for her as truly and
more fruitfully now than if fate had accepted the
offer then. Not only has his blood re-cemented
our Union, but the dignity, the patience, the self-
restraint, the thoughtfulness for others, the serene
valor which he showed under circumstances so disheartening and amid the wreck of hopes so splendid, are a possession and a stimulus to his countrymen forever. The emulation of examples like his
makes nations great, and keeps them so. The soil
out of which such men as he are made is good to
be born on, good to live on, good to die for and to
be buried in.

I had not the honor of any intimacy of friendship with this noble man. Others will speak of him
from more intimate knowledge. I saw him once or
twice only, but so deeply was I impressed with the
seriousness and solidity of his character, with his
eager interest in worthy objects, and with the
statesmanlike furniture of his mind, that when,
many years afterwards, he was nominated for the
Presidency I rejoiced in the wisdom of the selection, and found in my memory an image of him
clearer than that of any man I ever met of whom
I had seen so little. And I may add that I have
never known any man concerning whom a loving
and admiring testimony was so uniform from men
of every rank and character who had known him.

> " None knew him but to love him,
> None named him but to praise."

I shall not retrace the story of his life, but there is nothing that occurs to me so perfect in its completeness since the Biblical story of Joseph. The poor lad who at thirteen could not read dies at fifty the tenant of an office second in dignity to none on earth, and the world mourns his loss as that of a personal relative. I find the word coming back to my lips in spite of me, "He was so *human*." An example of it was his kissing his venerable mother on the day of his inauguration. It was criticised, I remember hearing at the time, as a sin against good taste. I thought then, and think now, that if we had found the story in Plutarch we should have thought no worse of the hero of it.

It was this pliability of his to the impulse of unconventional feeling that endeared him so much to his kind. Among the many stories that have been sent me, illustrating the sorrow so universally felt here, none have touched me so much as these two: An old gardener said to his mistress, " Oh, ma'am, we felt somehow as if he belonged to us;" and in a little village on the coast, where an evangelist held nightly services on the beach, prayer was offered regularly for the recovery of the President, the weather-beaten fishermen who stood around the preacher with bowed, uncovered heads fervently responding, "Amen." You will also be interested to know that the benevolent Sir Moses Montefiore, now in his ninety-seventh year, telegraphed last week to Palestine to request that prayers might be offered for the President in the synagogues of the four holy cities. It was no common man who could call forth, and justly call forth, an emotion so universal, an interest so sincere and so humane.

I said that this is no place for eulogy. They who deserve eulogy do not need it, and they who deserve it not are diminished by it. The dead at least can bear the truth, and have a right to that highest service of human speech. We are not called upon here to define Garfield's place among the memorable of mankind. A great man is made up of qualities that meet or make great occasions. We may surely say of him that the great qualities were there, and were always adequate to the need, although, less fortunate than Lincoln, his career was snapped short just as they were about to be tested by the supreme trial of creative statesmanship. We believe that he would have stood the test, and we have good reason for our faith. For this is certainly true of him, that a life more strenuous, a life of more constantly heightening tendency of fulfilment, of more salutary and invigorating example, has not been lived in a country that is rich in instances of such. Well may we be proud of him, this brother of ours, recognized also as a brother wherever men honor what is praiseworthy in man. Well may we thank God for him, and love more the country that could produce and appreciate him. Well may we sorrow for his loss, but not as those without hope. Great as the loss is — and the loss of faculties trained like his is the hardest of all to replace — yet we should show a want of faith in our country if we called it irreparable. Three times within living memory has the

Vice-President succeeded to the presidential function without shock to our system, without detriment to our national honor, and without check to our prosperity. It would be an indignity to discuss here the character of him who is now our chief magistrate, and who, more than any one, it is safe to say, has felt the pain of this blow. But there is no indecorum in saying what is known to all, that he is a gentleman of culture, of admittedly high intelligence, of unimpeachable character, of proved administrative ability, and that he enters on his high duties with a full sense of what such a succession implies. I am not one of those who believe that democracy any more than any other form of government will go of itself. I am not a believer in perpetual motion in politics any more than in mechanics, but, in common with all of you, I have an imperturbable faith in the honesty, the intelligence, and the good sense of the American people, and in the destiny of the American Republic.

STANLEY

SPEECH AT THE MEETING IN THE CHAPTER HOUSE OF
WESTMINSTER ABBEY IN COMMEMORATION OF DEAN
STANLEY, 13 DECEMBER, 1881.

I AM very glad to have the privilege of uniting
in this tribute to the memory of the remarkable
man whose loss was felt as a personal bereavement
by so great and so various a multitude of mourners, and, as has been so well said by his successor,
a multitude of mourners which included many who
had never seen his face. I feel especially happy
because it seems to me that my presence here is
an augury of that day, which may be distant, but
which I believe will surely come, when the character and services of every eminent man of the
British race in every land, under whatever distant
skies he may have been born, shall be the common
possession and the common inheritance and the
common pride of every branch which is sprung
from our ancestral stem. As I look round upon
this assembly, I feel that I may almost be pardoned
if I apply again the well-known line, —

> "Si monumentum requiris, circumspice."

The quality and the character of this meeting are
in themselves a monument and a eulogy. It would

be out of place for me to attempt any characteriza-
tion of Dean Stanley in the presence of those so
much more fitted than myself for the task ; but I
may be allowed to say a few words from the point
of view of a stranger.   I remember, on the day of
the Dean's funeral, what struck me as most remarkable was seeing all ranks and conditions of
men equalized, all differences of creed obliterated,
all animosities of sect and party appeased by the
touch of that common sympathy in sorrow.   The
newspapers, as was natural and proper, remarked
upon the number of distinguished persons who were
present.   To me, it seemed vastly more touching
to look upon the number of humble and undistin-
guished persons, who felt that their daily lives had
lost a consolation and their hearts a neighbor and
a friend.   If I were to put in one word what struck
me as perhaps the leading characteristic of Dean
Stanley, and what made him so dear to many, I
should say it was not his charity, though his charity was large, — for charity has in it sometimes,
perhaps often, a savor of superiority ; it was not
his toleration, — for toleration, I think, is apt to
make a concession of what should be simply recognized as a natural right, — but it was rather, as
it seems to me, the wonderful many-sidedness of his
sympathies.   I remember my friend Dr. Holmes,
whose name I am sure is known, and if known is
dear to most of you, called my attention to an epitaph in the neighborhood of Boston, in New England.   It recorded the name and date of the death
of a wife and mother, and then added simply, "She

was so pleasant." That always struck me in Dean Stanley. I think no man ever lived who was so pleasant to so many people. We visited him as we visit a clearer sky and a warmer climate. In thinking of this meeting this morning, I was reminded of a proverbial phrase which we have in America, and which, I believe, we carried from England : we apologize for the shortcomings and faults of our fellow-beings by saying, " There is a great deal of human nature in man." I think the one leading characteristic of Dean Stanley — and I say it to his praise — was the amount of human nature there was in him. So sweet, so gracious, so cheerful, so illuminating was it that there could not have been too much of it. It brought him nearer to all mankind, it recognized and called out the humanity that was in other men. His sympathies were so wide that they could not be confined by the boundaries of the land in which he was born : they crossed the channel and they crossed the ocean. No man was a foreigner to him, far less any American. And, in supporting the resolution, I should be inclined to make only one amendment : it would be to propose that the memorial, instead of being national, should be international. Since I came into the room, I have heard from Sir Rutherford Alcock that he has received from Boston, through the hands of Rev. Phillips Brooks, a friend of Dean Stanley, a contribution of £206 toward the Stanley Hall. I am sure I am not pledging my countrymen to too much when I say that they will delight to share in this tribute

to the late Dean.   And England has lately given
them, in so many ways, such touching and cordial
reasons for believing that they cannot enter as
strangers to any sorrow of hers, that I am sure you
will receive most substantial and most sympathetic
help from your kindred people on the other side of
the Atlantic, with whom the bonds of sympathy
have been lately drawn more close, and by nothing
more strikingly than by the sympathy expressed,
sir, by your Royal Mother, in a way which touched
every heart on the other side of the Atlantic, and
has called forth repeated expressions of gratitude.
It will give me great pleasure to do all I can to aid
the enterprise which is started here to-day.

FIELDING

ADDRESS ON UNVEILING THE BUST OF FIELDING, DE-
LIVERED AT SHIRE HALL, TAUNTON, SÓMERSETSHIRE,
ENGLAND, 4 SEPTEMBER, 1883.

I SHOULD have preferred that this office I am to
perform to-day had fallen to another. Especially
does it seem fitting that an English author should
take the first place in doing honor to the most
thoroughly English of writers; and yet there is
something very pleasant to me in thinking that
my presence here to-day bears witness to the union
of our tongue and of our literary traditions. I
seem to be not inappropriately verifying the prophecy of Samuel Daniel made nearly three centuries
ago : —

> " And who in time knows whither we may vent
> The treasure of our tongue, to what strange shores
> The gain of our best glory may be sent
> To enrich unknowing nations with our stores ?
> What worlds in the yet unformed Occident
> May come refined with accents that are ours ? "

I wish that I could hope to repay some part, however small, of this obligation by any accents of
mine. A whisper will ever and anon make itself
heard by the inward ear of literary men, asking
the importunate questions, "Pray, do you not
ascribe a rather disproportionate relative impor-

tance to the achievements of those of your own craft?" and "Does not genius manifest itself in many other ways, and those of far more practical usefulness to mankind?" No doubt an over-estimate of ourselves and of our own doings is a very common human failing, as we are all ready to admit when we candidly consider our neighbors, and yet the world is led by a true instinct to agree with us in assigning to works of imagination a usefulness higher in kind than any other, and in allowing to their authors a certain right of sanctuary in our affections, within whose limit the ordinary writs of human censure do not run ; for not only are the most vivid sensations of which our moral and intellectual nature is capable received through the imagination, but that mysterious faculty, in its loftiest and purest exercise, rescues us from our narrow personality, and lifts us up to regions of serener scope and more ideal satisfaction. It cheats us with a semblance of creative power that seems almost divine, and exhilarates us by a momentary enlargement of the boundaries of our conscious being, as if we had been brought into some nearer relationship with elemental forces. This magic, it is true, is wrought to the full only by the three or four great poets, and by them only in their finest and most emancipated moments. Well may we value this incomparable gift; well may we delight to honor the men who were its depositaries and instruments. Homer and Æschylus, and Dante and Shakespeare, speak to us as to their contemporaries, with an authority accumulated by all the

years between them and us, and with a voice whose
very remoteness makes it seem more divinely
clear. At the height which these men were sometimes capable of reaching, the processes of the
mind seem to be intuitive. But sometimes we find
our treasure in more earthen vessels; sometimes
this wonder-working faculty is bestowed upon men
whose natural and congenial element is the prose
of cities and the conventionalized emotion of that
artificial life which we are pleased to call real.
Here it is forced to combine itself as best it may
with the understanding, and it attains its ends —
such lower ends as only are possible — through
observation and slowly hoarded experience. Even
then, though it may have lost its highest, it has not
lost all its charm nor all the potency of its sway;
for I am inclined to think that it is some form
or other, some degree or other, of this *vivida vis*
of imagination which breaks the fetters of men's
self-consciousness for a while, and enables them to
play with their faculties instead of toiling with
them — gives them, in short, an indefinably delightful something that we call originality, or,
when it addresses itself to artistic creation, genius.
A certain sacredness was once attributed to the
builders of bridges and makers of roads, and we
but follow a natural and praiseworthy impulse
when we cherish the memory and record the worth
of any man of original and especially of creative
mind, since it is the office of such also to open the
highway for our fancy and our thought, through
the *chiaroscuro* of tangled actualities in which we

dwell, to commerce with fresh forms of nature
and new varieties of man.   It is the privilege of
genius that to it life never grows commonplace as
to the rest of us, and that it sees Falstaffs or Don
Quixotes or Squire Westerns where we have never
seen anything more than the ordinary Toms and
Dicks and Harries whom an inscrutable Providence
has seen fit to send into an already overpopu-
lated world.   These genius takes by the hand and
leads through a maze of imaginary adventures; ex-
poses to a cross-play of fictitious circumstances, to
the friction of other personages as unreal as themselves, and we exclaim " Why, they are alive; this
is creation!"   Yes, genius has endowed them with
a fulness of life, a completeness of being, such as
even they themselves had never dreamed of, and
they become truly citizens of the world forever.
A great living poet, who has in his own work illustrated every form of imagination, has told us admirably what the secret of this illusory creative-
ness is, as no one has a better right to know.

> " I find first
> Writ down for very a b c of fact,
> In the beginning God made heaven and earth,
> From which, no matter in what lisp, I spell
> And speak you out a consequence — that man —
> Man, as befits the made, the inferior thing,
> Purposed since made to grow, not make in turn;
> Yet forced to try and make, else fail to grow,
> Formed to rise, reach at, if not grasp and gain
> The good beyond him; which attempt is growth —
> Repeats God's process in man's due degree,
> A harmony man's proportionate result;
> Creates not, but resuscitates perhaps.
> No less man, bounded, yearning to be free,

May so project his surplusage of soul,
In search of body; so add self to self,
By owning what lay ownerless before,
So find, so fill full, so appropriate forms.
. . . Though nothing which had never life,
Shall get life from him, be, not having been,
Yet something dead may get to live again."

Now the man whom we are met to commemorate to-day felt this necessity and performed this feat, and his works are become a substantial part of that English literature which may be said not merely to exist, but to live. They have become so, among other reasons, because he had the courage to be absolutely sincere, if he had not always the tact to see where sincerity is out of place. We may discuss, we may estimate him, but we cannot push him from his place. His imagination was of that secondary order of which I have spoken, subdued to what it worked in; and his creative power is not less in degree than that of more purely ideal artists, but was different in kind, or, if not, is made to seem so by the more vulgar substance in which it wrought. He was inferior also in having no touch of tragic power or passion, though he can be pathetic when he will. There is nowhere a scene more pathetic than that of the supper Amelia prepares for Booth, who never comes to share it, and it is pathos made of materials as homely as Wordsworth himself would have chosen. Certainly Fielding's genius was incapable of that ecstasy of conception through which the poetic imagination seems fused into a molten unity with its material, and produces figures that are typical without loss of characteristic individuality, as if they were drawn, not from what we call real life, but from the very source of life itself, and were cast in that universal mould about which the subtlest thinkers that have ever lived so long busied them-selves. Fielding's characters are very real persons; but they are not types in the same sense as Lear and Hamlet. They seem to be men whom we have seen rather than men whom we might see if we were lucky enough, men who have been rather than who might have been. He was especially a humorist; and the weakness of the humorist is that he can never be quite unconscious, for in him it seems as if the two lobes of the brain were never in perfect unison, so that if ever one of them be on the point of surrendering itself to a fine frenzy of unqualified enthusiasm, the other watches it, makes fun of it, renders it uneasy with a vague sense of absurd incongruity, till at last it is forced to laugh when it had rather cry. Heine turned this to his purpose, and this is what makes him so profoundly, and yet sometimes so unpleasantly, pathetic. Shakespeare, as remarkable in this, perhaps, as in anything else, is the only man in whom the rarest poetic power has worked side by side at the same bench with humor, and has not been more or less disenchanted by it. I have lingered so long on general questions, not because I feared to meet more directly an objection which I am told has been made to this tribute of respect and affection for Fielding, but because I doubted whether it was necessary or wise to notice it at all; and yet, though it must be admitted that his books cannot be recommended *virginibus puerisque*, I will say frankly that it is not because they would corrupt, but because they would shock; and surely this need not affect the fact that he was a great and original genius who has done honor to his country, which is what we chiefly have to consider here. A gallery of Somersetshire worthies from which he was absent would be as incomplete as a history of English literature that should not mention him.

Fielding needs no recognition from us; his fame is established and admitted, and his character is gradually clearing itself of the stains with which malice or jealousy or careless hearsay had darkened it. It has become an established principle of criticism that in judging a man we must take into account the age in which he lived, and which was as truly a part of him as he of it. Fielding's genius has drawn forth the sympathetic commendation of such widely different men as Gibbon, Scott, Coleridge, Thackeray, and Leslie Stephen, and of such a woman as George Eliot. I possess a copy of "Tom Jones," the margins of which are crowded with the admiring comments of Leigh Hunt, as pure-minded a man as ever lived, and a critic whose subtlety of discrimination and whose soundness of judgment, supported as it was on a broad base of truly liberal scholarship, have hardly yet won fitting appreciation. There can be no higher testimonials to character than these; and lately Mr. Austin Dobson has done, perhaps, as true a service as one man of letters ever did to another by reducing what little is known of the life of Fielding from chaos to coherence by ridding it of fable, by correcting and coördinating dates, by cross-examining tradition till it stammeringly con- fessed that it had no visible means of subsistence, and has thus enabled us to get some authentic glimpse of the man as he really was. He has res- cued the body of Fielding from beneath the swinish hoofs which were trampling it as once they tram- pled the Knight of La Mancha, whom Fielding so heartily admired. We really know almost as little of Fielding's life as of Shakespeare's, but what we do know on any valid evidence is, I think, on the whole, highly creditable to him. Thrown upon the town at twenty with no training that would fit him for a profession, with the principles and tastes of the class to which he belonged by birth, and with a nominal allowance from his father of £200 a year, which, as he humorously said, "anybody might pay that would," it is possible that when he had money in his pocket he may have spent it in ways that he might blush to remember, and when his pocket was empty may have tried to replenish it by expedients that were not to his taste. But there is no proof of this except what is purely in- ferential, and there is evidence of the same kind, but stronger, that he had habits of study and in- dustry that are not to be put on at will as one puts on his overcoat, and that are altogether inconsis- tent with the dissolute life he is supposed to have led. The dramatic pieces that he wrote during his early period were, it is true, shamefully gross,

though there are humorous hints in them that have
been profitably worked up by later writers; but
what strikes me most in them is that there is so
little real knowledge of life, the result of personal
experience, and that the social scenery and conception of character are mainly borrowed from his immediate predecessors, the dramatists of the Restoration.   In grossness his plays could not outdo those
of Dryden, whose bust has stood so long without
protest in Westminster Abbey.   As to any harm
they can do there is little to be apprehended, for
they are mostly as hard to read as a Shapira manu-
script.   I do not deny that Fielding's temperament
was far from being over nice.   I am willing to admit, if you will, that the woof of his nature was
coarse and animal.   I should not stop short of saying that it was sensual.   Yet he liked and admired
the highest and best things of his time — the art of
Hogarth, the acting of Garrick, the verse of Pope.
He is said indeed to have loved low company, but
his nature was so companionable and his hunger
for knowledge so keen, that I fancy he would like
any society that was not dull, and any conversation, however illiterate, from which he could learn
anything to his purpose.   It may be suspected that
the polite conversation of the men of that day
would differ little, except in grammar, from the
talk of the pothouse.

As I have said, we must guard against falling
into the anachronism of forgetting the coarseness
of the age into which he was born, and whose atmosphere he breathed.   It was a generation whose

sense of smell was undisturbed by odors that would now evoke a sanitary commission, and its moral nostrils were of an equally masculine temper. A coarse thread shows itself here and there, even through the satiny surface of the fastidious Gray, and a taint of the century that gave him birth may be detected now and then in the "Doctor" of the pure and altogether admirable Southey. But it is objected that there is an immoral tendency in "Joseph Andrews," "Tom Jones," and "Amelia."

Certainly none of them is calculated to serve the cause of virtue, or at any rate of chastity, if measured by the standard of to-day. But as certainly that standard looks a little awkward in the hands of people who read George Sand and allow an expurgated edition of the Decalogue for the use of them that go in chariots. I confess that in my impatience of such criticism I feel myself tempted, when Fielding's muse shows a too liberal ankle, to cry out with Tam O'Shanter, "Weel dune, cutty sark!" His bluntness is more wholesome than the refinement of such critics, for the second of the Seven Deadly Sins is not less dangerous when she talks mysticism and ogles us through the gaps of a fan painted with the story of the Virgin Martyr. He did not go in search of impurity as if he relished the reek of it, like some French so-called realists for whose title-pages I should be inclined to borrow an inscription from the old tavern-signs, "Entertainment for Man — and Beast." He painted vice when it came in his way (and it was more obvious in his time) as a figure in the social landscape, and in doing so he was perhaps a better moralist than those who ignore it altogether, or only when it lives in a genteel quarter of the town. He at least does not paint the landscape as a mere background for the naked nymph. He never made the blunder of supposing that the Devil always smelt of sulphur. He thought himself to be writing history, and called' his novels Histories, as if to warn us that he should tell the whole truth without equivocation. He makes all the sins of his heroes react disastrously on their fortunes. He assuredly believed himself to be writing with an earnest moral purpose in his two greater and more deliberately composed works, and indeed clearly asserts as much. I also fully believe it, for the assertion is justified by all that we know of the prevailing qualities of his character, whatever may have been its failings and lapses, if failings and lapses they were. It does not seem to have occurred to the English clergyman who wrote the epitaph over his grave at Lisbon that there was any question about the matter, and he especially celebrates the moral purpose and effect of Fielding's works in Latin that would, perhaps, have made the subject of it a little uncomfortable. How, then, are we to explain certain scenes in these books, except by supposing that Fielding was utterly unconscious that there was any harm in them? Perhaps we might also say that he was so sincere a hater of cant and sham and hypocrisy that in his wrath against them he was not careful to consider the want of ceremonious decorum in his

protest, and forgot that frankness might stop short
of cynicism without losing any of its virtue. He
had so hearty an English contempt for sentimental-
ity that he did not always distinguish true sentiment from false, and setting perhaps an over-value
on manliness, looked upon refinement as the ornament and protection of womanly weakness rather
than as what it quite as truly is — the crown
and complement of manly strength. He admired
Richardson, and frankly expressed his admiration;
yet I think that over a bowl of punch he might
have misnamed him the "Homer of Boarding-
school Misses," just as Sainte-Beuve called Octave
Feuillet the "Alfred de Musset of Boarding-
schools."

But besides all this, Fielding was a naturalist, in
the sense that he was an instinctive and careful
observer. He loved truth, and, for an artist, seems
to have too often missed the distinction between
truth and exactitude. He forgot the warning of
Sir Walter Raleigh, perhaps more important to the
artist than to the historian, that it is dangerous to
follow truth too near the heels. His aim was to
paint life as he saw it, not as he wished it was or
hoped it might be; to show us what men really did,
not what they were pleased to believe they thought
it would be well for other men to do: and this
he did with a force, a directness, and a vividness
of coloring that make him in the truest sense a
painter of history. No one can fail to admit the
justice of the analogy between him and his friend
Hogarth in this respect, pointed out by Mr. Dob-

son. In both cases we may regret that their model was too often no better than she should be. In the case both of Tom Jones and of Booth, it is to be noted, so far as the moral purpose is concerned, that their lapse from virtue always draws after them a retribution which threatens ruin to their dearest desires. I think it was Thackeray who said that Fielding had dared to paint a man — an exploit for which no one would have the courage now.

This is not the place or occasion for a critical estimate of Fielding, even could one add anything of value to what has been already said by competent persons. If there were a recognized standard in criticism, as in apothecaries' measure, so that by adding a grain of praise to this scale, or taking away a scruple of blame from that, we could make the balance manifestly even in the eyes of all men, it might be worth while to weigh Hannibal; but when each of us stamps his own weights, and warrants the impartiality of his own scales, perhaps the experiment may be wisely foregone. Let it suffice here to state generally the reasons for which we set a high value on this man whose bust we unveil to-day. Since we are come together, not to judge, but only to commemorate, perhaps it would be enough to say, in justification of to-day's ceremony, that Fielding was a man of genius; for it is hardly once in a .century, if so often, that a whole country catches so rare and shy a specimen of the native fauna, and proportionably more seldom that a county is so lucky. But Fielding was something more even than this. It is not extravagant to say

that he marks an epoch, and that we date from
him the beginning of a consciously new form of
literature. It was not without reason that Byron,
expanding a hint given somewhere by Fielding
himself, called him "the prose Homer of human
nature." He had more than that superficial knowledge of literature which no gentleman's head
should be without. He knew it as a craftsman
knows the niceties and traditions of his craft. He
saw that since the epic in verse ceased to be recited
in the market-places, it had become an anachronism ; that nothing but the charm of narrative had
saved Ariosto, as Tasso had been saved by his
diction, and Milton by his style; but that since
Milton every epic had been born as dead as the
Pharaohs — more dead, if possible, than the "Co-
lumbiad" of Joel Barlow and the "Charlemagne"
of Lucien Bonaparte are to us. He saw that the
novel of actual life was to replace it, and he set
himself deliberately (after having convinced himself experimentally in Parson Adams that he could
create character) to produce an epic on the lower
and more neighborly level of prose. However
opinions may differ as to the other merits of "Tom
Jones," they are unanimous as to its harmony of
design and masterliness of structure.

Fielding, then, was not merely, in my judgment
at least, an original writer, but an originator. He
has the merit, whatever it may be, of inventing the
realistic novel, as it is called. I do not mean to say
that there had been no stories professedly of real
life before. The story of "Francion" is such, and

even more notably " Gil Blas," not to mention others. But before Fielding it seems to me that real life formed rather the scenic background than the substance, and that the characters are, after all, merely players who represent certain types rather than the living types themselves. Fielding, as a novelist, drew the motives that impel his characters in all their actions from human nature, and not from artificial life. When I read " Gil Blas," I do not become part of the story — I listen to an agreeable story-teller who narrates and describes, and I wait to hear what is going to happen ; but in Fielding I want to see what people are going to do and say, and I can half guess what will happen, because I know them and what they are and what they are likely to do. They are no longer images, but actual beings. Nothing can persuade me, for example, that I do not know the sound of Squire Western's voice.

Fielding did not and could not idealize, his object being exact truth, but he realized the actual truth around him as none had done before and few have done since. As a creator of characters that are actuated by a motive power within themselves, and that are so livingly real as to become our familiar acquaintances, he is among the greatest. Abraham Adams is excellent, and has had a numerous progeny, but I think that even he is inferior in originality, in coherence, and in the entire keeping of look, speech, motive, and action, to Squire Western, who is, indeed, one of the most simple and perfect creations of genius. If he has been less often copied than Parson Adams, may it not be because he is a more finished work of art, and, therefore, more difficult to copy? I need not expatiate on the simple felicity and courteousness of his style, the unobtrusive clothing of a thought as clear as it is often profound, or on the good-nature of his satire, in which he reminds one of Chaucer, or on the subtle gravity of his irony, more delicate than that of Swift, and, therefore, perhaps even more deadly. I will only say that I think it less perfect, because more obviously intentional, in " Jonathan Wild " than in such masterpieces as the account of Captain Blifil's death, and the epitaph upon his tomb. When it seems most casual and inadvertent, it often cuts deepest, as when Squire Western, impatient of Parson Supple's intervention, says to him, " Arn't in pulpit now ; when art a got up there then I never mind what dost say." I must not forget to say a word of his dialogue, which, except where he wishes to show off his attainments in classical criticism, as in some chapters of " Amelia," is altogether so admirably spirited and characteristic that it makes us wonder at his failure as a dramatist. We may read Fielding's character clearly in his books, for it was not complex, but especially in his " Voyage to Lisbon," where he reveals it in artless inadvertence. He was a lovingly thoughtful husband, a tender father, a good brother, a useful and sagacious magistrate. He was courageous, gentle, thoroughly conscious of his own dignity as a gentleman, and able to make that dignity respected. If we seek for a single characteristic which more than any other would sum him up, we should say that it was his absolute manliness, a manliness in its type English from top to toe.   It is eminently fitting, therefore, that the reproduction of his features, which I am about to unveil, should be from the hand of a woman.   Let me close with a quotation which was a favorite with Fielding : —

> " Verum ubi plura nitent, . . . non ego paucis
> Offendar maculis, quas aut incuria fudit,
> Aut humana parum cavit natura."

COLERIDGE

ADDRESS ON UNVEILING THE BUST OF COLERIDGE, IN
WESTMINSTER ABBEY, 7 MAY, 1885.

I SHOULD have preferred for many reasons, on
which I need not dwell, for they must be present
to the minds of all who hear me, that the duty I
have undertaken to perform here to-day had fallen
to other hands. But the fact that this memorial
of one who, if not a great poet and a great teacher,
had in him the almost over-abundant materials
of both, is the gift of one of my countrymen, the
late Rev. Dr. Mercer, of Newport, Rhode Island,
through his executrix, Mrs. Pell, seems to supply
that argument of fitness that would otherwise have
been absent. It does more, and for this I prize
it the more; it adds a fresh proof, if any were
needed, that not all the waters of that ocean which
divides but cannot divorce them can wash out of
the consciousness of either nation the feeling that
we hold our intellectual property in common, that
we own allegiance to the same moral and literary
traditions, and that the fame of those who have
shed lustre on our race, as it is an undivided inheritance, so it imposes an equal debt of gratitude,
an equal responsibility, on the two great branches
of it. Twice before I have had the honor of

speaking within the precincts of this structure, the
double sanctuary of religion and renown, surely
the most venerable of ecclesiastical buildings to
men of English blood. Once again I was a silent
spectator while his body was laid here to mingle
with consecrated earth who more deeply than any
other in modern times had penetrated with the
ferment of his thought the thinking of mankind,
an event of deep significance as the proclamation
of that truce between science and religion which
is, let us hope, the forerunner of their ultimate
reconciliation. When I spoke here it was in commemoration of personal friends, one of them the
late Dean Stanley, dear to all who knew him ; the
other an American poet, dear to all who speak the
English tongue. It is to commemorate another
friend that I come here to-day, for who so worthy
of the name as one who was our companion and
teacher in the happiest hours of our youth, made
doubly happy by the charm of his genius, and who
to our old age brings back, if not the presence, at
least the radiant image of the youth we have lost ?
Surely there are no friends so constant as the
poets, and among them, I think, none more faithful than Coleridge. I am glad to have a share in
this reparation of a long injustice, for as we looked
about us hitherto in Poet's Corner we were tempted
to ask, as Cavalcante dei Cavalcanti did of Dante,
If these are here through loftiness of genius, where
is he? It is just fifty-one years ago that I became the possessor of an American reprint of Ga-
lignani's edition of Coleridge, Shelley, and Keats

in one volume.   It was a pirated book, and I trust
I may be pardoned for the delight I had in it.   I
take comfort from the thought that there must be
many a Scottish minister and laird now in Heaven
who liked their claret none the less that it had paid
no tribute to the House of Hanover.   I have heard
this trinity of poets taxed with incongruity.   As
for me, I was grateful for such infinite riches in a
little room, and never thought of looking a Pegasus
in the mouth whose triple burden proved a stronger
back than that even of the Templars' traditional
steed.   Much later, but still long ago, I read the
"Friend," the "Biographia Literaria," and other
prose works of Coleridge.   In what may be given
me to say I shall be obliged to trust chiefly to a
memory which at my time of life is gradually becoming one of her own reminiscences, and is forced
to compound as best she may with her inexorable
creditor, Oblivion.   But perhaps she will serve me
all the better for the matter in hand, for what is
proper here is at most a rapid generalization rather
than a demonstration in detail of his claims to grateful remembrance.   I shall naturally trust myself to
judge him by his literary rather than by his meta-
physical achievement.   In the latter region I cannot
help being reminded of the partiality he so often be-
trays for clouds, and see him, to use his own words,
"making the shifting clouds seem what you please,"
or "a traveller go from mount to mount through
cloudland, gorgeous land."   Or sometimes I think
of him as an alchemist in search of the philosopher's stone, and stripping the lead, not only from

his own roof, but from that of the parish church itself, to quench the fiery thirst of his alembic. He seems never to have given up the hope of finding in the imagination some universal solvent, some *magisterium majus*, by which the lead of scepticism should be transmuted into the pure gold of faith, or, at least, persuaded to believe itself so. But we should not forget that many earnest and superior minds found his cloud castles solid habitations, nor that alchemy was the nursing mother of chemistry. He certainly was a main influence in showing the English mind how it could emancipate itself from the vulgarizing tyranny of common sense, and teaching it to recognize in the imagination an important factor not only in the happiness but in the destiny of man. In criticism he was, indeed, a teacher and interpreter whose service was incalculable. He owed much to Lessing, something to Schiller, and more to the younger Schlegel, but he owed most to his own sympathetic and penetrative imagination. This was the lifted torch (to borrow his own words again) that bade the starry walls of passages, dark before to the apprehension of even the most intelligent reader, sparkle with a lustre, latent in them to be sure, but not all their own. As Johnson said of Burke, he wound into his subject like a serpent. His analysis was elucidative mainly, if you will, but could not have been so except in virtue of the processes of constructive and philosophical criticism that had gone on so long in his mind as to make its subtle apprehension seem an instinct.

As he was the first to observe some of the sky's appearances and some of the shyer revelations of outward nature, so he was also first in noting some of the more occult phenomena of thought and emotion. It is a criticism of parts and passages, and was scattered carelessly in *obiter dicta*, but it was not a bringing of the brick as a specimen of the whole house. It was comparative anatomy, far rather, which from a single bone reconstructs the entire living organism. Many of his hints and suggestions are more pregnant than whole treatises, as where he says that the wit of Hudibras is the wit of thought.

But what I think constitutes his great power, as it certainly is his greatest charm, is the perpetual presence of imagination, as constant a quality with him as fancy is with Calderon. She was his life-long housemate, if not always hanging over his shoulders and whispering in his ear, yet within easy call, like the Abra of Prior —

> "Abra was with him ere he spoke her name,
> And if he called another, Abra came."

It was she who gave him that power of sympathy which made his Wallenstein what I may call the most original translation in our language, unless some of the late Mr. Fitzgerald's be reckoned such. He was not exact any more than Chapman. The molten material of his mind, too abundant for the capacity of the mould, overflowed it in gushes of fiery excess. But the main object of translation he accomplishes. Poetry is reproduced as poetry, and genius shows itself as genius, patent even in

the march of the verse. As a poet, the impression
he made upon his greater contemporaries will, I
believe, be the ultimate verdict of criticism. They
all thought of him what Scott said of him, "No
man has all the resources of poetry in such profusion. . . . His fancy and diction would long ago
have placed him above all his contemporaries had
they been under the direction of a sound judgment
and a steady will." No doubt we have in Coleridge the most striking example in literature of a
great genius given in trust to a nerveless will and
a fitful purpose. But I think the secret of his
doing no more in poetry is to be found in the fact
that the judgment, so far from being absent, grew
to be there in excess. His critical sense rose like
a forbidding apparition in the path of his poetic
production. I have heard of a military engineer
who knew so well how a bridge should be built that
he could never build one. It certainly was not
wholly indolence that was to blame in Coleridge's
case, for though he used to say early in life that he
had no "finger industry," yet he left behind him a
mass of correspondence, and his letters are generally long. But I do not care to discuss a question
the answer to which must be left mainly to conjecture or to the instinct of individual temperament.
It is enough for us here that he has written some
of the most poetical poetry in the language, and
one poem, the "Ancient Mariner," not only unparalleled, but unapproached in its kind, and that
kind of the rarest. It is marvellous in its mastery
over that delightfully fortuitous inconsequence that

is the adamantine logic of dreamland. Coleridge has taken the old ballad measure and given to it by an indefinable charm wholly his own all the sweetness, all the melody and compass of a symphony. And how picturesque it is in the proper sense of the word. I know nothing like it. There is not a description in it. It is all picture. Descriptive poets generally confuse us with multiplicity of detail; we cannot see their forest for the trees; but Coleridge never errs in this way. With instinctive tact he touches the right chord of association, and is satisfied, as we also are. I should find it hard to explain the singular charm of his diction, there is so much nicety of art and purpose in it, whether for music or meaning. Nor does it need any explanation, for we all feel it. The words seem common words enough, but in the order of them, in the choice, variety, and position of the vowel-sounds they become magical. The most decrepit vocable in the language throws away its crutches to dance and sing at his piping. I cannot think it a personal peculiarity, but a matter of universal experience, that more bits of Coleridge have imbedded themselves in my memory than of any other poet who delighted my youth — unless I should except the sonnets of Shakespeare. This argues perfectness of expression. Let me cite an example or two : —

> "The sun's rim dips, the stars rush out,
>   At one stride comes the dark;
>   With far-heard whisper through the dark
>   Off shot the spectre barque."

Or take this as a bit of landscape : —

> " Beneath yon birch with silver bark
> And boughs so pendulous and fair,
> The brook falls scattered down the rock,
> And all is mossy there."

It is a perfect little picture and seems so easily done. But try to do something like it. Coleridge's words have the unashamed nakedness of Scripture, of the Eden of diction ere the voluble serpent had entered it. This felicity of speech in Coleridge's best verse is the more remarkable because it was an acquisition. His earlier poems are apt to be turgid, in his prose there is too often a languor of profuseness, and there are pages where he seems to be talking to himself and not to us, as I have heard a guide do in the tortuous caverns of the Catacombs when he was doubtful if he had not lost his way. But when his genius runs freely and full in his prose, the style, as he said of Pascal, " is a garment of light." He knew all our best prose and knew the secret of its composition. When he is well inspired, as in his best poetry he commonly is, he gives us the very quintessence of perception, the clearly crystallized precipitation of all that is most precious in the ferment of impression after the impertinent and obtrusive particulars have evaporated from the memory. It is the pure visual ecstasy disengaged from the confused and confusing material that gave it birth. It seems the very beatitude of artless simplicity, and is the most finished product of art. I know nothing so perfect in its kind since Dante. The tiny landscape I have cited reminds me in its laconic adequacy of —

" Li ruscelletti che de' verdi colli
Del Casentin discendon giuso in Arno,
Faccendo i lor canali e freddi e molli."

I confess that I prefer the " Ancient Mariner" to
"Christabel," fine as that poem is in parts and
tantalizing as it is in the suggestion of deeper
meanings than were ever there. The " Ancient
Mariner " seems to have come of itself. In " Christabel " I fancy him saying, " Go to, let us write an
imaginative poem." It never could be finished on
those terms.

This is not the time nor the place to pass judgment on Coleridge the man. Doubtless it would
have been happier for him had he been endowed
with the business faculty that makes his friend
Wordsworth so almost irritatingly respectable.
But would it have been happier for us? We are
here to-day not to consider what Coleridge owed
to himself, to his family, or to the world, but what
we owe to him. Let us at least not volunteer to
draw his frailties from their dread abode. Our
own are a far more profitable subject of contemplation. Let the man of imaginative temperament,
who has never procrastinated, who has made all
that was possible of his powers, cast the first stone.
The cairn, I think, will not be as tall as Hector's.
With Coleridge I believe the opium to have been
congenital, and if we may judge by many a profoundly pathetic cry both in his poems and his letters, he answered grievously for his frailties during
the last thirty years of his life. In an unpublished
letter of his he says, speaking of another, but

thinking certainly of himself, " An unfortunate man, enemy to himself only, and like all of that character expiating his faults by suffering beyond what the severest judge would have inflicted as their due punishment." There let us leave it, for nothing is more certain than that our personal weaknesses exact the uttermost farthing of penalty from us while we live. Even in the dilapidation of his powers, due chiefly, if you will, to his own unthrifty management of them, we might, making proper deductions, apply to him what Mark Antony says of the dead Cæsar —

> " He was the ruins of the noblest man
> That ever lived in the tide of time."

Whatever may have been his faults and weaknesses, he was the man of all his generation to whom we should most unhesitatingly allow the distinction of genius, that is, of one authentically possessed from time to time by some influence that made him better and greater than himself. If he lost himself too much in what Mr. Pater has admirably called "impassioned contemplation," he has at least left us such a legacy as only genius, and genius not always, can leave. It is for this that we pay him this homage of memory. He himself has said that —

> " It seems like stories from the land of spirits
> If any man obtain that which he merits,
> Or any merit that which he attains."

Both conditions are fulfilled to-day.

BOOKS AND LIBRARIES

ADDRESS AT THE OPENING OF THE FREE PUBLIC LI-
BRARY IN CHELSEA, MASSACHUSETTS, 22 DECEMBER,
1885.

A FEW years ago my friend, Mr. Alexander Ireland, published a very interesting volume which he
called " The Book-Lover's Enchiridion," the hand-
book, that is to say, of those who love books. It
was made up of extracts from the writings of a
great variety of distinguished men, ancient and
modern, in praise of books. It was a chorus of
many voices in many tongues, a hymn of gratitude
and praise, full of such piety and fervor as can be
paralleled only in songs dedicated to the supreme
Power, the supreme Wisdom, and the supreme
Love. Nay, there is a glow of enthusiasm and sincerity in it which is often painfully wanting in
those other too commonly mechanical compositions.
We feel at once that here it is out of the fulness
of the heart, yes, and of the head, too, that the
mouth speaketh. Here was none of that compulsory commonplace which is wont to characterize
those " testimonials of celebrated authors," by
means of which publishers sometimes strive to
linger out the passage of a hopeless book toward
its *requiescat* in oblivion. These utterances which
Mr. Ireland has gathered lovingly together are

stamped with that spontaneousness which is the mint-mark of all sterling speech. It is true that they are mostly, as is only natural, the utterances of literary men, and there is a well-founded proverbial distrust of herring that bear only the brand of the packer, and not that of the sworn inspector. But to this objection a cynic might answer with the question, "Are authors so prone, then, to praise the works of other people that we are to doubt them when they do it unasked?" Perhaps the wisest thing I could have done to-night would have been to put upon the stand some of the more weighty of this cloud of witnesses. But since your invitation implied that I should myself say something, I will endeavor to set before you a few of the commonplaces of the occasion, as they may be modified by passing through my own mind, or by having made themselves felt in my own experience.

The greater part of Mr. Ireland's witnesses testify to the comfort and consolation they owe to books, to the refuge they have found in them from sorrow or misfortune, to their friendship, never estranged and outliving all others. This testimony they volunteered. Had they been asked, they would have borne evidence as willingly to the higher and more general uses of books in their service to the commonwealth, as well as to the individual man. Consider, for example, how a single page of Burke may emancipate the young student of politics from narrow views and merely contemporaneous judgments. Our English ancestors, with that common-sense which is one of the most useful,

though not one of the most engaging, properties
of the race, made a rhyming proverb, which says
that —

> " When land and goods are gone and spent,
> *Then* learning is most excellent ; "

and this is true so far as it goes, though it goes perhaps hardly far enough. The law also calls only
the earth and what is immovably attached to it *real*
property, but I am of opinion that those only are
real possessions which abide with a man after he
has been stripped of those others falsely so called,
and which alone save him from seeming and from
being the miserable forked radish to which the bit-
ter scorn of Lear degraded every child of Adam.
The riches of scholarship, the benignities of literature defy fortune and outlive calamity. They are
beyond the reach of thief or moth or rust. As they
cannot be inherited, so they cannot be alienated.
But they may be shared, they may be distributed,
and it is the object and office of a free public
library to perform these beneficent functions.

"Books," says Wordsworth, " are a real world,"
and he was thinking, doubtless, of such books as are
not merely the triumphs of pure intellect, however
supreme, but of those in which intellect infused
with the sense of beauty aims rather to produce delight than conviction, or, if conviction, then through
intuition rather than formal logic, and, leaving
what Donne wisely calls —

> " Unconcerning things matters of fact "

to science and the understanding, seeks to give
ideal expression to those abiding realities of the

spiritual world for which the outward and visible
world serves at best but as the husk and symbol.
Am I wrong in using the word *realities?* wrong in
insisting on the distinction between the real and
the actual? in assuming for the ideal an existence
as absolute and self subsistent as that which appeals to our senses, nay, so often cheats them, in
the matter of fact? How very small a part of
the world we truly live in is represented by what
speaks to us through the senses when compared
with that vast realm of the mind which is peopled
by memory and imagination, and with such shining
inhabitants! These walls, these faces, what are
they in comparison with the countless images, the
innumerable population which every one of us can
summon up to the tiny show-box of the brain, in
material breadth scarce a span, yet infinite as space
and time? and in what, I pray, are those we gravely
call historical characters, of which each new historian strains his neck to get a new and different
view, in any sense more real than the personages of
fiction? Do not serious and earnest men discuss
Hamlet as they would Cromwell or Lincoln? Does
Cæsar, does Alaric, hold existence by any other or
stronger tenure than the Christian of Bunyan or
the Don Quixote of Cervantes or the Antigone of
Sophocles? Is not the history which is luminous
because of an indwelling and perennial truth to nature, because of that light which never was on land
or sea, really *more* true, in the highest sense, than
many a weary chronicle with names and date and
place in which " an Amurath to Amurath suc-

ceeds "? Do we know as much of any authentic
Danish prince as of Hamlet?

But to come back a little nearer to Chelsea and
the occasion that has called us together. The
founders of New England, if sometimes, when they
found it needful, an impracticable, were always a
practical people. Their first care, no doubt, was
for an adequate supply of powder, and they encouraged the manufacture of musket bullets by enact-
ing that they should pass as currency at a farthing
each — a coinage nearer to its nominal value and
not heavier than some with which we are familiar.
Their second care was that " good learning should
not perish from among us," and to this end they at
once established the Grammar (Latin) School in
Boston, and soon after the college at Cambridge.
The nucleus of this was, as you all know, the be-
quest in money by John Harvard. Hardly less
important, however, was the legacy of his library,
a collection of good books, inconsiderable measured
by the standard of to-day, but very considerable
then as the possession of a private person. From
that little acorn what an oak has sprung, and from
its acorns again what a vocal forest, as old Howell
would have called it, — old Howell whom I love to
cite, because his name gave their title to the " Essays of Elia," and is borne with slight variation
by one of the most delightful of modern authors.
It was, in my judgment, those two foundations,
more than anything else, which gave to New England character its bent, and to Boston that literary
supremacy which, I am told, she is in danger of

losing, but which she will not lose till she and all the world lose Holmes.

The opening of a free public library, then, is a most important event in the history of any town. A college training is an excellent thing ; but, after all, the better part of every man's education is that which he gives himself, and it is for this that a good library should furnish the opportunity and the means. I have sometimes thought that our public schools undertook to teach too much, and that the older system, which taught merely the three R's, and taught them well, leaving natural selection to decide who should go farther, was the better. However this may be, all that is primarily needful in order to use a library is the ability to read. I say primarily, for there must also be the inclination, and, after that, some guidance in reading well. Formerly the duty of a librarian was considered too much that of a watch-dog, to keep people as much as possible away from the books, and to hand these over to his successor as little worn by use as he could. Librarians now, it is pleasant to see, have a different notion of their trust, and are in the habit of preparing, for the direction of the inexperienced, lists of such books as they think best worth reading. Cataloguing has also, thanks in great measure to American librarians, become a science, and catalogues, ceasing to be labyrinths without a clue, are furnished with finger-posts at every turn. Subject catalogues again save the beginner a vast deal of time and trouble by supplying him for nothing with one at least of the

results of thorough scholarship, the knowing where
to look for what he wants. I do not mean by this
that there is or can be any short cut to learning,
but that there may be, and is, such a short cut to
information that will make learning more easily
accessible.

But have you ever rightly considered what the
mere ability to read means? That it is the key
which admits us to the whole world of thought and
fancy and imagination? to the company of saint
and sage, of the wisest and the wittiest at their
wisest and wittiest moment? That it enables us to
see with the keenest eyes, hear with the finest ears,
and listen to the sweetest voices of all time? More
than that, it annihilates time and space for us; it
revives for us without a miracle the Age of Wonder, endowing us with the shoes of swiftness and
the cap of darkness, so that we walk invisible
like fern-seed, and witness unharmed the plague at
Athens or Florence or London; accompany Cæsar
on his marches, or look in on Catiline in council with his fellow conspirators, or Guy Fawkes
in the cellar of St. Stephen's. We often hear of
people who will descend to any servility, submit to
any insult, for the sake of getting themselves or
their children into what is euphemistically called
good society. Did it ever occur to them that there
is a select society of all the centuries to which they
and theirs can be admitted for the asking, a society, too, which will not involve them in ruinous
expense and still more ruinous waste of time and
health and faculties?

Southey tells us that, in his walk one stormy day, he met an old woman, to whom, by way of greeting, he made the rather obvious remark that it was dreadful weather. She answered, philosophically, that, in her opinion, " *any* weather was better than none ! " I should be half inclined to say that any reading was better than none, allaying the crudeness of the statement by the Yankee proverb, which tells us that, though " all deacons are good, there 's odds in deacons." Among books, certainly, there is much variety of company, ranging from the best to the worst, from Plato to Zola, and the first lesson in reading well is that which teaches us to distinguish between literature and merely printed matter. The choice lies wholly with ourselves. We have the key put into our hands; shall we unlock the pantry or the oratory ? There is a Wallachian legend which, like most of the figments of popular fancy, has a moral in it. One Bakála, a good-for-nothing kind of fellow in his way, having had the luck to offer a sacrifice especially well pleasing to God, is taken up into heaven. He finds the Almighty sitting in something like the best room of a Wallachian peasant's cottage — there is always a profound pathos in the homeliness of the popular imagination, forced, like the princess in the fairy tale, to weave its semblance of gold tissue out of straw. On being asked what reward he desires for the good service he has done, Bakála, who had always passionately longed to be the owner of a bagpipe, seeing a half worn-out one lying among some rubbish in a corner of the room, begs eagerly that it may be bestowed on him. The Lord, with a smile of pity at the meanness of his choice, grants him his boon, and Bakála goes back to earth delighted with his prize. With an infinite possibility within his reach, with the choice of wisdom, of power, of beauty at his tongue's end, he asked according to his kind, and his sordid wish is answered with a gift as sordid. Yes, there is a choice in books as in friends, and the mind sinks or rises to the level of its habitual society, is subdued, as Shakespeare says of the dyer's hand, to what it works in. Cato's advice, *cum bonis ambula*, consort with the good, is quite as true if we extend it to books, for they, too, insensibly give away their own nature to the mind that converses with them. They either beckon upwards or drag down. *Du gleichst dem Geist den du begreifst*, says the World Spirit to Faust, and this is true of the ascending no less than of the descending scale. Every book we read may be made a round in the ever-lengthening ladder by which we climb to knowledge and to that temperance and serenity of mind which, as it is the ripest fruit of Wisdom, is also the sweetest. But this can only be if we read such books as make us think, and read them in such a way as helps them to do so, that is, by endeavoring to judge them, and thus to make them an exercise rather than a relaxation of the mind. Desultory reading, except as conscious pastime, hebetates the brain and slackens the bow-string of Will. It communicates as little intelligence as the messages that run along the telegraph wire to the

birds that perch on it.   Few men learn the highest
use of books.   After lifelong study many a man
discovers too late that to have had the philosopher's
stone availed nothing without the philosopher to
use it.   Many a scholarly life, stretched like a talking wire to bring the wisdom of antiquity into
communion with the present, can at last yield us
no better news than the true accent of a Greek
verse, or the translation of some filthy nothing
scrawled on the walls of a brothel by some Pom-
peian idler.   And it is certainly true that the material of thought reacts upon the thought itself.
Shakespeare himself would have been commonplace
had he been paddocked in a thinly shaven vocabulary, and Phidias, had he worked in wax, only a
more inspired Mrs. Jarley.   A man is known, says
the proverb, by the company he keeps, and not
only so, but made by it.   Milton makes his fallen
angels grow small to enter the infernal council
room, but the soul, which God meant to be the spa-
cious chamber where high thoughts and generous
aspirations might commune together, shrinks and
narrows itself to the measure of the meaner company that is wont to gather there, hatching conspiracies against our better selves.   We are apt to
wonder at the scholarship of the men of three centuries ago and at a certain dignity of phrase that
characterizes them.   They were scholars because
they did not read so many things as we.   They had
fewer books, but these were of the best.   Their
speech was noble, because they lunched with Plutarch and supped with Plato.   We spend as much

time over print as they did, but instead of communing with the choice thoughts of choice spirits, and unconsciously acquiring the grand manner of that supreme society, we diligently inform ourselves, and cover the continent with a cobweb of telegraphs to inform us, of such inspiring facts as that a horse belonging to Mr. Smith ran away on Wednesday, seriously damaging a valuable carryall; that a son of Mr. Brown swallowed a hickory nut on Thursday; and that a gravel bank caved in and buried Mr. Robinson alive on Friday. Alas, it is we ourselves that are getting buried alive under this avalanche of earthy impertinences! It is we who, while we might each in his humble way be helping our fellows into the right path, or adding one block to the climbing spire of a fine soul, are willing to become mere sponges saturated from the stagnant goosepond of village gossip. This is the kind of news we compass the globe to catch, fresh from Bungtown Centre, when we might have it fresh from heaven by the electric lines of poet or prophet! It is bad enough that we should be compelled to know so many nothings, but it is downright intolerable that we must wash so many barrow-loads of gravel to find a grain of mica after all. And then to be told that the ability to read makes us all shareholders in the Bonanza Mine of Universal Intelligence!

One is sometimes asked by young people to recommend a course of reading. My advice would be that they should confine themselves to the supreme books in whatever literature, or still better to choose some one great author, and make themselves thoroughly familiar with him. For, as all roads lead to Rome, so do they likewise lead away from it, and you will find that, in order to understand perfectly and weigh exactly any vital piece of literature, you will be gradually and pleasantly persuaded to excursions and explorations of which you little dreamed when you began, and will find yourselves scholars before you are aware. For remember that there is nothing less profitable than scholarship for the mere sake of scholarship, nor anything more wearisome in the attainment. But the moment you have a definite aim, attention is quickened, the mother of memory, and all that you acquire groups and arranges itself in an order that is lucid, because everywhere and always it is in intelligent relation to a central object of constant and growing interest. This method also forces upon us the necessity of thinking, which is, after all, the highest result of all education. For what we want is not learning, but knowledge ; that is, the power to make learning answer its true end as a quickener of intelligence and a widener of our intellectual sympathies. I do not mean to say that every one is fitted by nature or inclination for a definite course of study, or indeed for serious study in any sense. I am quite willing that these should " browse in a library," as Dr. Johnson called it, to their hearts' content. It is, perhaps, the only way in which time may be profitably wasted. But desultory reading will not make a " full man," as Bacon understood it, of one who has not Johnson's memory, his power of assimilation, and, above all, his comprehensive view of the relations of things. "Read not," says Lord Bacon, in his Essay of Studies, " to contradict and confute ; nor to believe and take for granted ; nor to find talk and discourse ; but to weigh and consider. Some books are to be tasted, others to be swallowed, and some few to be chewed and digested ; that is, some books are to be read only in parts ; others to be read, but not curiously [carefully], and some few to be read wholly and with diligence and attention. *Some books also may be read by deputy.*" This is weighty and well said, and I would call your attention especially to the wise words with which the passage closes. The best books are not always those which lend themselves to discussion and comment, but those (like Montaigne's Essays) which discuss and comment ourselves.

I have been speaking of such books as should be chosen for profitable reading. A public library, of course, must be far wider in its scope. It should contain something for all tastes, as well as the material for a thorough grounding in all branches of knowledge. It should be rich in books of reference, in encyclopædias, where one may learn without cost of research what things are generally known. For it is far more useful to know these than to know those that are *not* generally known. Not to know them is the defect of those half-trained and therefore hasty men who find a mare's nest on every branch of the tree of knowledge. A library should contain ample stores of history, which, if it do not

always deserve the pompous title which Boling-
broke gave it, of philosophy teaching by example,
certainly teaches many things profitable for us to
know and lay to heart; teaches, among other things,
how much of the present is still held in mortmain
by the past; teaches that, if there be no controlling purpose, there is, at least, a sternly logical sequence in human affairs, and that chance has but
a trifling dominion over them; teaches why things
are and must be so and not otherwise, and that,
of all hopeless contests, the most hopeless is that
which fools are most eager to challenge — with the
Nature of Things; teaches, perhaps, more than
anything else, the value of personal character as a
chief factor in what used to be called destiny, for
that cause is strong which has not a multitude,
but one strong man behind it. History is, indeed,
mainly the biography of a few imperial men, and
forces home upon us the useful lesson how infini-
tesimally important our own private affairs are to
the universe in general. History is clarified experience, and yet how little do men profit by it; nay,
how should we expect it of those who so seldom are
taught anything by their own! Delusions, especially economical delusions, seem the only things
that have any chance of an earthly immortality. I
would have plenty of biography. It is no insignificant fact that eminent men have always loved their
Plutarch, since example, whether for emulation or
avoidance, is never so poignant as when presented
to us in a striking personality. Autobiographies
are also instructive reading to the student of human

nature, though generally written by men who are
more interesting to themselves than to their fellow men.   I have been told that Emerson and
George Eliot agreed in thinking Rousseau's " Con-
fessions " the most interesting book they had ever
read.

A public library should also have many and full
shelves of political economy, for the dismal science,
as Carlyle called it, if it prove nothing else, will go
far towards proving that theory is the bird in the
bush, though she sing more sweetly than the nightingale, and that the millennium will not hasten its
coming in deference to the most convincing string
of resolutions that were ever unanimously adopted
in public meeting.   It likewise induces in us a profound and wholesome distrust of social panaceas.

I would have a public library abundant in translations of the best books in all languages, for,
though no work of genius can be adequately translated, because every word of it is permeated with
what Milton calls " the precious life-blood of a
master spirit " which cannot be transfused into the
veins of the best translation, yet some acquaintance
with foreign and ancient literatures has the liber-
alizing effect of foreign travel.   He who travels by
translation travels more hastily and superficially,
but brings home something that is worth having,
nevertheless.   Translations properly used, by short-
ening the labor of acquisition, add as many years
to our lives as they subtract from the processes of
our education.   Looked at from any but the æsthetic point of view, translations retain whatever

property was in their originals to enlarge, liberalize, and refine the mind. At the same time I would have also the originals of these translated books as a temptation to the study of languages, which has a special use and importance of its own in teaching us to understand the niceties of our mother tongue. The practice of translation, by making us deliberate in the choice of the best equivalent of the foreign word in our own language, has likewise the advantage of continually schooling us in one of the main elements of a good style, — precision ; and precision of thought is not only exemplified by precision of language, but is largely dependent on the habit of it.

In such a library the sciences should be fully represented, that men may at least learn to know in what a marvellous museum they live, what a wonder-worker is giving them an exhibition daily for nothing. Nor let Art be forgotten in all its many forms, not as the antithesis of Science, but as her elder or fairer sister, whom we love all the more that her usefulness cannot be demonstrated in dollars and cents. I should be thankful if every day-laborer among us could have his mind illumined, as those of Athens and of Florence had, with some image of what is best in architecture, painting, and sculpture, to train his crude perceptions and perhaps call out latent faculties. I should like to see the works of Ruskin within the reach of every artisan among us. For I hope some day that the delicacy of touch and accuracy of eye that have made our mechanics in some departments the best in the world, may give us the same supremacy in works of wider range and more purely ideal scope.

Voyages and travels I would also have, good store, especially the earlier, when the world was fresh and unhackneyed and men saw things invisible to the modern eye. They are fast sailing ships to waft away from present trouble to the Fortunate Isles.

To wash down the drier morsels that every library must necessarily offer at its board, let there be plenty of imaginative literature, and let its range be not too narrow to stretch from Dante to the elder Dumas. The world of the imagination is not the world of abstraction and nonentity, as some conceive, but a world formed out of chaos by a sense of the beauty that is in man and the earth on which he dwells. It is the realm of Might-be, our haven of refuge from the shortcomings and disillusions of life. It is, to quote Spenser, who knew it well —

"The world's sweet inn from care and wearisome turmoil."

Do we believe, then, that God gave us in mockery this splendid faculty of sympathy with things that are a joy forever? For my part, I believe that the love and study of works of imagination is of practical utility in a country so profoundly material (or, as we like to call it, practical) in its leading tendencies as ours. The hunger after purely intellectual delights, the content with ideal possessions, cannot but be good for us in maintaining a wholesome balance of the character and of the faculties. I for one shall never be persuaded that Shakespeare left a less useful legacy to his countrymen than Watt. We hold all the deepest, all the highest satisfactions of life as tenants of imagination. Nature will keep up the supply of what are called hard-headed people without our help, and, if it come to that, there are other as good uses for heads as at the end of battering rams.

I know that there are many excellent people who object to the reading of novels as a waste of time, if not as otherwise harmful. But I think they are trying to outwit nature, who is sure to prove cunninger than they. Look at children. One boy shall want a chest of tools, and one a book, and of those who want books one shall ask for a botany, another for a romance. They will be sure to get what they want, and we are doing a grave wrong to their morals by driving them to do things on the sly, to steal that food which their constitution craves and which is wholesome for them, instead of having it freely and frankly given them as the wisest possible diet. If we cannot make a silk purse out of a sow's ear, so neither can we hope to succeed with the opposite experiment. But we may spoil the silk for its legitimate uses. I can conceive of no healthier reading for a boy, or girl either, than Scott's novels, or Cooper's, to speak only of the dead. I have found them very good reading at least for one young man, for one middle-aged man, and for one who is growing old. No, no — banish the Antiquary, banish

Leather Stocking, and banish all the world! Let us not go about to make life duller than it is.

But I must shut the doors of my imaginary library or I shall never end. It is left for me to say a few words of cordial acknowledgment to Mr. Fitz for his judicious and generous gift. I have great pleasure in believing that the custom of giving away money during their lifetime (and there is nothing harder for most men to part with, except prejudice) is more common with Americans than with any other people. It is a still greater pleasure to see that the favorite direction of their beneficence is towards the founding of colleges and libraries. My observation has led me to believe that there is no country in which wealth is so sensible of its obligations as our own. And, as most of our rich men have risen from the ranks, may we not fairly attribute this sympathy with their kind to the benign influence of democracy rightly understood? My dear and honored friend, George William Curtis, told me that he was sitting in front of the late Mr. Ezra Cornell in a convention, where one of the speakers made a Latin quotation. Mr. Cornell leaned forward and asked for a translation of it, which Mr. Curtis gave him. Mr. Cornell thanked him, and added, " If I can help it, no young man shall grow up in New York hereafter without the chance, at least, of knowing what a Latin quotation means when he hears it." This was the germ of Cornell University, and it found food for its roots in that sympathy and thoughtfulness for others of which I just

spoke. This is the healthy side of that good nature which democracy tends to foster, and which is
so often harmful when it has its root in indolence
or indifference; especially harmful where our public affairs are concerned, and where it is easiest,
because there we are giving away what belongs to
other people. It should be said, however, that in
this country it is as laudably easy to procure signa-
tures to a subscription paper as it is shamefully so
to obtain them for certificates of character and
recommendations to office. And is not this public
spirit a national evolution from that frame of mind
in which New England was colonized, and which
found expression in these grave words of Robinson
and Brewster: "We are knit together as a body
in a most strict and sacred bond and covenant of
the Lord, of the violation of which we make great
conscience, and by virtue whereof we hold ourselves strictly tied to all care of each other's good,
and of the whole." Let us never forget the deep
and solemn import of these words. The problem
before us is to make a whole of our many discordant parts, our many foreign elements, and I know
of no way in which this can better be done than by
providing a common system of education and a
common door of access to the best books by which
that education may be continued, broadened, and
made fruitful. For it is certain that, whatever we
do or leave undone, those discordant parts and
foreign elements are to be, whether we will or no,
members of that body which Robinson and Brewster had in mind, bone of our bone, and flesh of our

flesh, for good or ill. I am happy in believing that democracy has enough vigor of constitution to assimilate these seemingly indigestible morsels and transmute them into strength of muscle and symmetry of limb.

There is no way in which a man can build so secure and lasting a monument for himself as in a public library. Upon that he may confidently allow " Resurgam " to be carved, for, through his good deed, he will rise again in the grateful remembrance and in the lifted and broadened minds and fortified characters of generation after generation. The pyramids may forget their builders, but memorials such as this have longer memories.

Mr. Fitz has done his part in providing your library with a dwelling. It will be for the citizens of Chelsea to provide it with worthy habitants. So shall they, too, have a share in the noble eulogy of the ancient wise man: "The teachers shall shine as the firmament, and they that turn many to righteousness as the stars forever and ever."

WORDSWORTH

ADDRESS AS PRESIDENT OF THE WORDSWORTH SOCIETY,
10 MAY, 1884.

In an early volume of the " Philosophical Transactions " there is a paper concerning " A certain
kind of Lead found in Germany proper for Essays."
That it may have been first found in Germany I
shall not question, but deposits of this depressing
mineral have been discovered since in other countries also, and we are all of us more or less familiar
with its presence in the essay, — nowhere more
than when this takes the shape of a critical dis-
sertation on some favorite poet.   Is this, then,
what poets are good for, that we may darken them
with our elucidations, or bury them out of sight
under the gathering silt of our comments?   Must
we, then, peep and botanize on the rose of dawn
or the passion-flower of sunset?   I should rather
take the counsel of a great poet, the commentaries
on whom already make a library in themselves, and
say, —

   " State contenti, umana gente, al *quia*,"

be satisfied if poetry be delightful, or helpful, or
inspiring, or all these together, but do not consider too nicely why it is so.

I would not have you suppose that I am glancing covertly at what others, from Coleridge down, have written of Wordsworth. I have read them, including a recent very suggestive contribution of Mr. Swinburne, with no other sense of dissatisfaction than that which springs from "desiring this man's art and that man's scope." No, I am thinking only that whatever can be profitably or unprofitably said of him has been already said, and that what is said for the mere sake of saying it is not worth saying at all. Moreover, I myself have said of him what I thought good more than twenty years ago.[1] It is as wearisome to repeat one's self as it is profitless to repeat others, and that we have said something, however inadequate it may afterwards seem to us, is a great hindrance to saying anything better.

The only function that a president of the Wordsworth Society is called on to perform is that of bidding it farewell at the end of his year, and it is perhaps fortunate that I have not had the leisure to prepare a discourse so deliberate as to be more worthy of the occasion. Without unbroken time there can be no consecutive thought, and it is my misfortune that in the midst of a reflection or of a sentence I am liable to be called away by the bell of private or public duty. Even had I been able to prepare something that might have satisfied me better, I should still be at the disadvantage of following next after a retiring president[2] who always

---

[1] *Literary Essays*, iv. 354.
[2] Mr. Matthew Arnold.

has the art of saying what all of us would be glad
to say if we could, and who in his address last year
gave us what seemed to me the finished model of
what such a performance should be.

During the year that has passed since our last
Annual Meeting, however idle the rest of us may
have been, our secretary has been fruitfully busy,
and has given us two more volumes of what it is safe
to say will be the standard and definitive edition
of the poet's works. In this, the chronological
arrangement of the several poems, and still more
the record in the margin of the author's corrections
or repentances (*pentimenti*, as the Italians prettily
call them), furnish us with a kind of self-register-
ing instrument of the exactest kind by which to
note, if not always the growth of his mind, yet certainly the gradual clarification of his taste, and the
somewhat toilsome education of his ear. It is
plain that with Wordsworth, more than with most
poets, poetry was an art, — an art, too, rather painfully acquired by one who was endowed by nature
with more of the vision than of the faculty divine.
Some of the more important omissions, especially,
seem silently to indicate changes of opinion, though
oftener, it may be suspected, of mood, or merely a
shifting of the point of view, the natural conse-
quence of a change for the better in his own material condition.

One result of this marshalling of the poems by
the natural sequence of date is the conviction that,
whatever modifications Wordsworth's ideas concerning certain social and political questions may

have undergone, these modifications had not their
origin in inconsiderate choice, or in any seduction
of personal motive, but were the natural and unconscious outcome of enlarged experience, and of
more profound reflection upon it. I see no reason
to think that he ever swerved from his early faith
in the beneficence of freedom, but rather that he
learned the necessity of defining more exactly in
what freedom consisted, and the conditions, whether
of time or place, under which alone it can be beneficent, of insisting that it must be an evolution and
not a manufacture, and that it should coördinate
itself with the prior claims of society and civilization. The process in his mind was the ordinary
crystallization of sentiment hitherto swimming in
vague solution, and now precipitated in principles.
He had made the inevitable discovery that comes
with years, of how much harder it is to do than to
see what 't were good to do, and grew content to
build the poor man's cottage, since the means did
not exist of building the prince's palace he had
dreamed. It is noticeable how many of his earlier
poems turn upon the sufferings of the poor from
the injustice of man or the unnatural organization
of society. He himself had been the victim of an
abuse of the power that rank and wealth sometimes put into the hands of unworthy men, and
had believed in political methods, both for remedy
and prevention. He had believed also in the
possibility of a gregarious regeneration of man by
sudden and sharp, if need were by revolutionary
expedients, like those impromptu conversions of

the inhabitants of a city from Christ to Mahomet, or back again, according to the creed of their conqueror, of which we read in mediæval romances. He had fancied that the laws of the universe would curtsy to the resolves of the National Convention. He had seen this hope utterly baffled and confuted, as it seemed, by events in France, by events that had occurred, too, in the logical sequence foretold by students of history. He had been convinced, perhaps against his will, that a great part of human suffering has its root in the nature of man, and not in that of his institutions. Where was the remedy to be found, if remedy indeed there were? It was to be sought at least only in an improvement wrought by those moral influences that build up and buttress the personal character. Goethe taught the self-culture that results in self-possession, in breadth and impartiality of view, and in equipoise of mind; Wordsworth inculcated that self-development through intercourse with man and nature which leads to self-sufficingness, self-sustainment, and equilibrium of character. It was the individual that should and could be leavened, and through the individual the lump. To reverse the process was to break the continuity of history and to wrestle with the angel of destiny.

And for one of the most powerfully effective of the influences for which he was seeking, where should he look if not to Religion? The sublimities and amenities of outward nature might suffice for William Wordsworth, might for him have almost filled the place of a liberal education; but they

elevate, teach, and above all console the imaginative and solitary only, and suffice to him who already suffices to himself.   The thought of a god
vaguely and vaporously dispersed throughout the
visible creation, the conjecture of an animating
principle that gives to the sunset its splendors, its
passion to the storm, to cloud and wind their sympathy of form and movement, that sustains the
faith of the crag in its forlorn endurance, and of
the harebell in the slender security of its stem,
may inspire or soothe, console or fortify, the man
whose physical and mental fibre is so sensitive that,
like the spectroscope, it can both feel and record
these impalpable impulses and impressions, these
impersonal vibrations of identity between the frag-
mentary life that is in himself and the larger life
of the universe whereof he is a particle.   Such
supersensual emotions might help to make a poem,
but they would not make a man, still more a social
being.   Absorption in the whole would not tend to
that development of the individual which was the
corner-stone of Wordsworth's edifice.

That instinct in man which leads him to fashion
a god in his own image, why may it not be an instinct as natural and wholesome as any other?
And it is not only God that this instinct embodies
and personifies, but every profounder abstract conception, every less selfish devotion of which man is
capable.   Was it, think you, of a tiny crooked out-
line on the map, of so many square miles of earth,
or of Hume and Smollett's History that Nelson
was thinking when he dictated what are perhaps

the most inspiring words ever uttered by an Englishman to Englishmen? Surely it was something in woman's shape that rose before him with all the potent charm of noble impulsion that is hers as much through her weakness as her strength. And the features of that divine apparition, had they not been painted in every attitude of their changeful beauty by Romney?

Coarse and rudimentary as this instinct is in the savage, it is sublimed and etherealized in the profoundly spiritual imagination of Dante, which yet is forced to admit the legitimacy of its operation. Beatrice tells him —

> "Thus to your minds it needful is to speak,
> Because through sense alone they understand:
> It is for this that Scripture condescends
> Unto your faculties, and feet and hands
> To God attributes, meaning something else."

And in what I think to be the sublimest reach to which poetry has risen, the conclusion of the "Paradiso," Dante tells us that within the three whirling rings of vari-colored light that symbolize the wisdom, the power, and the love of God, he seems to see the image of man.

Wordsworth would appear to have been convinced that this Something deeply interfused, this pervading but illusive intimation, of which he was dimly conscious, and that only by flashes, could never serve the ordinary man, who was in no way and at no time conscious of it, as motive, as judge, and more than all as consoler, — could never fill the place of the Good Shepherd. Observation con-

vinced him that what are called the safeguards of
society are the staff also of the individual members
of it; that tradition, habitude, and heredity are
great forces, whether for impulse or restraint. He
had pondered a pregnant phrase of the poet Daniel,
where he calls religion " mother of Form and
Fear." A growing conviction of its profound truth
turned his mind towards the Church as the embod-
iment of the most potent of all traditions, and to
her public offices as the expression of the most
socially humanizing of all habitudes. It was no
empty formalism that could have satisfied his conception, but rather that " Ideal Form, the universal
mould," that *forma mentis æterna* which has given
shape and expression to the fears and hopes and
aspirations of mankind. And what he understood
by Fear is perhaps shadowed forth in the " Ode to
Duty," in which he speaks to us out of an ampler
ether than in any other of his poems, and which
may safely " challenge insolent Greece and haughty
Rome " for a comparison either in kind or degree.

I ought not to detain you longer from the interesting papers, the reading of which has been prom-
ised for this meeting. No member of this Society
would admit that its existence was needed to keep
alive an interest in the poet, or to promote the
study of his works. But I think we should all consent that there could be no better reason for its
being than the fact that it elicits an utterance of
the impression made by his poetry on many different minds looking at him from as many different
points of view. That he should have a special

meaning for every one in an audience so various in temperament and character might well induce us to credit him with a wider range of sympathies and greater breadth of thought than each of us separately would, perhaps, be ready to admit.

But though reluctant to occupy more than my fair share of your time, the occasion tempts me irresistibly to add a few more words of general criticism. It has seemed to me that Wordsworth has too commonly been estimated rather as philosopher or teacher than as poet. The value of what he said has had more influence with the jury than the way in which he said it. There are various methods of criticism, but I think we should all agree that literary work is to be judged from the purely literary point of view.

If it be one of the baser consolations, it is also one of the most disheartening concomitants of long life, that we get used to everything. Two things, perhaps, retain their freshness more perdurably than the rest, — the return of spring, and the more poignant utterances of the poets. And here, I think, Wordsworth holds his own with the best. But Mr. Arnold's volume of selections from him suggests a question of some interest, for the Wordsworth Society of special interest, — How much of his poetry is likely to be a permanent possession? The answer to this question is involved in the answer to a question of wider bearing, — What are the conditions of permanence? Immediate or contemporaneous recognition is certainly not dominant among them, or Cowley would still be popular, —

Cowley, to whom the Muse gave every gift but one, the gift of the unexpected and inevitable word. Nor can mere originality assure the interest of posterity, else why are Chaucer and Gray familiar, while Donne, one of the subtlest and most self-irradiating minds that ever sought an outlet in verse, is known only to the few? Since Virgil there have been at most but four cosmopolitan authors, — Dante, Cervantes, Shakespeare, and Goethe. These have stood the supreme test of being translated into all tongues, because the large humanity of their theme, and of their handling of it, needed translation into none. Calderon is a greater poet than Goethe, but even in the most masterly translation he retains still a Spanish accent, and is accordingly *interned* (if I may Anglicize a French word) in that provincialism which we call nationality.

When one reads what has been written about Wordsworth, one cannot fail to be struck by the predominance of the personal equation in the estimate of his value, and when we consider his claim to universal recognition, it would not be wise to overlook the rare quality of the minds that he has most attracted and influenced. If the character of the constituency may be taken as the measure of the representative, there can be no doubt that, by his privilege of interesting the highest and purest order of intellect, Wordsworth must be set apart from the other poets, his contemporaries, if not above them. And yet we must qualify this praise by the admission that he continues to be insular;

that he makes no conquests beyond the boundaries of his mother-tongue; that, more than perhaps any other poet of equal endowment, he is great and surprising in passages and ejaculations. In these he truly

> " Is happy as a lover, and attired
> In sudden brightness, like a man inspired ; "

in these he loses himself, as Sir Thomas Browne would say, in an *O, altitudo*, where his muse is indeed a muse of fire, that can ascend, if not to the highest heaven of invention, yet to the supremest height of impersonal utterance. Then, like Elias the prophet, " he stands up as fire, and his word burns like a lamp." But too often, when left to his own resources, and to the conscientious performance of the duty laid upon him to be a great poet *quand même*, he seems diligently intent on producing fire by the primitive method of rubbing the dry sticks of his blank verse one against the other, while we stand in shivering expectation of the flame that never comes. In his truly inspired and inspiring passages it is remarkable also that he is most unlike his ordinary self, least in accordance with his own theories of the nature of poetic expression. When at his best, he startles and waylays as only genius can, but is furthest from that equanimity of conscious and constantly indwelling power that is the characteristic note of the greatest work. If Wordsworth be judged by the *ex ungue leonem* standard, by passages, or by a dozen single poems, no one capable of forming an opinion would hesitate to pronounce him, not only a great poet, but among the greatest, convinced in the one case by the style, and in both by the force that radiates from him, by the stimulus he sends kindling through every fibre of the intellect and of the imagination. At the same time there is no admittedly great poet in placing whom we are forced to acknowledge so many limitations and to make so many concessions.

Even as a teacher he is often too much of a pedagogue, and is apt to forget that poetry instructs not by precept and inculcation, but by hints and indirections and suggestions, by inducing a mood rather than by enforcing a principle or a moral. He sometimes impresses our fancy with the image of a schoolmaster whose class-room commands an unrivalled prospect of cloud and mountain, of all the pomp and prodigality of heaven and earth. From time to time he calls his pupils to the window, and makes them see what, without the finer intuition of his eyes, they had never seen; makes them feel what, without the sympathy of his more penetrating sentiment, they had never felt. It seems the revelation of a new heaven and a new earth, and to contain in itself its own justification. Then suddenly recollecting his duty, he shuts the window, calls them back to their tasks, and is equally well pleased and more discursive in enforcing on them the truth that the moral of all this is that in order to be happy they must be virtuous. If the total absence of any sense of humor had the advantage sometimes of making Wordsworth sublimely unconscious, it quite as often made him so to his loss.

In his noblest utterances man is absent except
as the antithesis that gives a sharper emphasis to
nature. The greatest poets, I think, have found
man more interesting than nature, have considered
nature as no more than the necessary scenery, ar-
tistically harmful if too pompous or obtrusive, before which man acts his tragi-comedy of life. This
peculiarity of Wordsworth results naturally from
the fact that he had no dramatic power, and of narrative power next to none. If he tell us a story,
it is because it gives him the chance to tell us something else, and to him of more importance. In
Scott's narrative poems the scenery is accessary
and subordinate. It is a picturesque background
to his figures, a landscape through which the action
rushes like a torrent, catching a hint of color perhaps from rock or tree, but never any image so dis-
tinct that it tempts us aside to reverie or medita-
tion. With Wordsworth the personages are apt
to be lost in the landscape, or kept waiting idly
while the poet muses on its deeper suggestions.
And he has no sense of proportion, no instinct of
choice and discrimination. All his thoughts and
emotions and sensations are of equal value in his
eyes because they are his, and he gives us methodi-
cally and conscientiously all he can, and not that
only which he cannot help giving because it must
and will be said. One might apply to him what
Miss Skeggs said of Dr. Burdock, that "he seldom
leaves anything out, as he writes only for his own
amusement." There is no limit to his — let us call
it facundity. He was dimly conscious of this, and

turned by a kind of instinct, I suspect, to the sonnet, because its form forced boundaries upon him, and put him under bonds to hold his peace at the end of the fourteenth line. Yet even here nature would out, and the oft-recurring *same subject continued* lures the nun from her cell to the convent parlor, and tempts the student to make a pulpit of his pensive citadel. The hour-glass is there, to be sure, with its lapsing admonition, but it reminds the preacher only that it can be turned.

I have said that Wordsworth was insular, but, more than this, there is also something local, I might say parochial, in his choice of subject and tone of thought. I am not sure that what is called philosophical poetry ever appeals to more than a very limited circle of minds, though to them it appeals with an intimate power that makes them fanatical in their preference. Perhaps none of those whom I have called universal poets (unless it be Dante) calls out this fanaticism, for they do not need it, fanaticism being a sure token either of weakness in numbers or of weakness in argument. The greatest poets interest the passions of men no less than their intelligence, and are more concerned with the secondary than the primal sympathies, with the concrete than with the abstract.

But I have played the *advocatus diaboli* long enough. I come back to the main question from which I set out. Will Wordsworth survive, as Lucretius survives, through the splendor of certain sunbursts of imagination refusing for a passionate moment to be subdued by the unwilling material in which it is forced to work, while that material takes fire in the working as it can and will only in the hands of genius, as it cannot and will not, for example, in the hands of Dr. Akenside? Is he to be known a century hence as the author of remarkable passages? Certainly a great part of him will perish, not, as Ben Jonson said of Donne, for want of understanding, but because too easily understood. His teaching, whatever it was, is part of the air we breathe, and has lost that charm of exclusion and privilege that kindled and kept alive the zeal of his acolytes while it was still sectarian, or even heretical. But he has that surest safeguard against oblivion, that imperishable incentive to curiosity and interest that belongs to all original minds. His finest utterances do not merely nestle in the ear by virtue of their music, but in the soul and life, by virtue of their meaning. One would be slow to say that his general outfit as poet was so complete as that of Dryden, but that he habitually dwelt in a diviner air, and alone of modern poets renewed and justified the earlier faith that made poet and prophet interchangeable terms. Surely he was not an artist in the strictest sense of the word; neither was Isaiah; but he had a rarer gift, the capability of being greatly inspired. Popular, let us admit, he can never be; but as in Catholic countries men go for a time into retreat from the importunate dissonances of life to collect their better selves again by communion with things that are heavenly, and therefore eternal, so this Chartreuse of Wordsworth, dedicated to the Genius of Solitude, will allure to its imperturbable calm the finer natures and the more highly tempered intellects of every generation, so long as man has any intuition of what is most sacred in his own emotions and sympathies, or of whatever in outward nature is most capable of awakening them and making them operative, whether to console or strengthen. And over the entrance-gate to that purifying seclusion shall be inscribed, —

> "Minds innocent and quiet take
> This for an hermitage."

DON QUIXOTE

NOTES READ AT THE WORKINGMEN'S COLLEGE, GREAT
ORMOND STREET, LONDON.

IN every literature which can be in any sense
called national there is a flavor of the soil from
which it sprang, in which it grew, and from which
its roots drew nourishment. This flavor, at first,
perhaps, the cause of distaste, gives a peculiar relish
when we have once learned to like it. It is a limi-
tation, no doubt, and when artificially communicated, or in excess, incurs the reproach of provincialism, just as there are certain national dishes
that are repugnant to every foreign palate. But
it has the advantage of giving even to second-class
writers in a foreign language that strangeness
which in our own tongue is possible only to originality either of thought or style. When this savor
of nationality is combined with original genius, as
in such a writer as Calderon, for example, the
charm is incalculably heightened.

Spanish literature, if it have nothing that for
height and depth can be compared with the " Di-
vina Commedia " of Dante (as indeed what other
modern literature has?), is rich in works that will
repay study, and evolved itself by natural processes
out of the native genius, the history, and the min-

gled races of the country more evidently, perhaps,
than that of any other modern people. It was of
course more or less modified from time to time by
foreign, especially by French, influences in its earlier period, by Italian in the sixteenth century, and
in later times again by French and German influences more or less plainly marked, but through
all and in spite of all, by virtue of the vigor of its
native impulse, it has given an essentially Spanish
character to all its productions. Its earliest monument, the " Song of the Cid," is in form a reproduction of the French " Chanson de Geste," a song
of action or of what has been acted, but the spirit
which animates it is very different from that which
animates the " Song of Roland," its nearest French
parallel in subject and form. The Spanish Romances, very much misrepresented in the spirited
and facile reproductions of Lockhart, are beyond
question the most original and fascinating popular
poetry of which we know anything. Their influence upon the form of Heine's verse is unmistaka-
ble. In the Drama, also, Spain has been especially
abundant and inventive. She has supplied all
Europe with plots, and has produced at least one
dramatist who takes natural rank with the greatest
in any language by his depth of imagination and
fertility of resource. For fascination of style and
profound suggestion, it would be hard to name another author superior to Calderon, if indeed equal
to him. His charm was equally felt by two minds
as unlike each other as those of Goethe and Shelley. These in themselves are sufficient achieve-

ments, and the intellectual life of a nation could maintain itself on the unearned increment of these without further addition to its resources. But Spain has also had the good fortune to produce one book which by the happiness of its conception, by the variety of its invention, and the charm of its style, has been adopted into the literature of mankind, and has occupied a place in their affection to which few other books have been admitted.

We have no word in English so comprehensive as the *Dichtung* of the Germans, which includes every exercise of the creative faculty, whether in the line of pathos or humor, whether in the higher region of imagination or on the lower levels of fancy where the average man draws easier breath. It is about a work whose scene lies on this inferior plane, but whose vividness of intuition and breadth of treatment rank it among the highest achievements of imaginative literature, that I shall say a few words this evening, and I trust that I shall see nothing in it that in the author's intention, at least, is not honestly to be found there; certainly that I shall not pretend to see anything which others have professed to discover there, but to which nature has made me color-blind.

I ask your attention not to an essay on "Don Quixote," still less to an essay on Cervantes, but rather to a few illustrative comments on his one immortal book (drawn almost wholly from notes written on its margin in repeated readings), which may tend to throw a stronger light on what I shall not scruple to call its incomparable originality both as a conception and a study of character. It is one of the few books that can lay undisputed claim to the distinction of being universal and cosmopolitan, equally at home in all languages and welcome to all kindreds and conditions of men; a *human* book in the fullest sense of the word; a kindly book, whether we take that adjective in its original meaning of *natural*, or in its present acceptation, which would seem to imply that at some time or other, not too precisely specified in history, to be kindly and to be natural had been equivalent terms. I can think of no book so thoroughly good-natured and good-humored; and this is the more remarkable because it shows that the optimism of its author had survived more misfortune and disenchantment than have fallen to the lot of many men, even the least successful. I suspect that Cervantes, with his varied experience, maimed at the battle of Lepanto, a captive in Algiers, pinched with poverty all his life, and writing his great book in a debtor's prison, might have formed as just an estimate of the vanity of vanities as the author of the Book of Ecclesiastes. But the notion of *Weltschmerz*, or the misery of living and acting in this beautiful world, seems never to have occurred to him, or, if it did, never to have embittered him. Had anybody suggested the thought to him, he would probably have answered, " Well, perhaps it is not the best of all possible worlds, but it is the best we have, or are likely to get in *my* time. Had I been present at its creation, I might, perhaps, as Alfonso the Learned thought *he* might, have given some useful advice for its improvement, and, were I consulted even now, could suggest some amendments in my own condition therein. But after all, it is not a bad world, as worlds go, and the wisest plan, if the luck go against us, is to follow the advice of Durandarte in the Cave of Montesinos, ' Patience, and shuffle the cards.' A new deal may give us better hands." His sense of humor kept his nature sweet and fresh, and made him capable of seeing that there are two sides to every question, even to a question in which his own personal interest was directly involved. In his dedication of the Second Part of " Don Quixote " to the Conde de Lemos, written in old age and infirmity, he smiles cheerfully on Poverty as on an old friend and lifelong companion. St. Francis could not have looked with more benignity on her whom he chose, as Dante tells us, for his bride.

I have called " Don Quixote " a cosmopolitan book, and I know of none other that can compete with it in this respect unless it be " Robinson Crusoe." But " Don Quixote," if less verisimilar as a narrative, and I am not sure that it is, appeals to far higher qualities of mind and demands a far subtler sense of appreciation than the masterpiece of Defoe. If the latter represent in simplest prose what interests us because it *might* happen to any man, the other, while seeming never to leave the low level of fact and possibility, constantly suggests the loftier region of symbol, and sets before us that eternal contrast between the ideal and the

real, between the world as it might be and the
world as it is, between the fervid completeness of
conception and the chill inadequacy of fulfilment,
which life sooner or later, directly or indirectly,
forces upon the consciousness of every man who is
more than a patent digester. There is a moral in
" Don Quixote," and a very profound one, whether
Cervantes consciously put it there or not, and it is
this: that whoever quarrels with the Nature of
Things, wittingly or unwittingly, is certain to get
the worst of it. The great difficulty lies in finding
out what the Nature of Things really and perdurably is, and the great wisdom, after we have made
this discovery, or persuaded ourselves that we have
made it, is in accommodating our lives and actions
to it as best we may or can. And yet, though all
this be true, there is another and deeper moral in
the book than this. The pathos which underlies its
seemingly farcical turmoil,[1] the tears which sometimes tremble under our lids after its most poignant touches of humor, the sympathy with its hero
which survives all his most ludicrous defeats and
humiliations and is only deepened by them, the
feeling that he is after all the one noble and heroic
figure in a world incapable of comprehending him,

[1] I can think of no better instance to show how thin is the
partition that divides humor from pathos than the lustration of the
two vulgar Laises (distraidas mozas) by the pure imagination of
Don Quixote (Part. Prim. cap. ii.). The sentiment is more natural and truer than that which Victor Hugo puts into the mouth of
Marion Delorme when she tells her lover that " his love has given
her back her maidenhood." To *him* it might, but it would rather
have reproached her with the loss of it.

and to whose inhabitants he is distorted and cari-
catured by the crooked panes in those windows of
custom and convention through which they see
him, all this seems to hint that only he who has
the imagination to conceive and the courage to
attempt a trial of strength with what foists itself
on our senses as the Order of Nature for the time
being, can achieve great results or kindle the co-
operative and efficient enthusiasm of his fellowmen.
The Don Quixote of one generation may live to hear
himself called the savior of society by the next.
How exalted was Don Quixote's own conception of
his mission is clear from what is said of his first
sight of the inn,[1] that " it was as if he had seen a
star which guided him not to the portals, but to the
fortress of his redemption," where the allusion were
too daring were he not persuaded that he is going
forth to redeem the world. Cervantes, of course, is
not so much speaking in his own person, as telling
what passed in the mind of his hero. But he would
not have ventured such an allusion in jest.

Am I forcing upon Cervantes a meaning alien
to the purpose of his story and anachronistic to the
age in which he lived? I do not think so, and if I
err I do so in good company. I admit that there
is a kind of what is called constructive criticism,
which is sometimes pushed so far beyond its proper
limits as to deserve rather the name of destructive,
as sometimes, in the so-called restoration of an ancient building, the materials of the original architect
are used in the erection of a new edifice of which he

[1] Part. Prim. cap. iii.

had never dreamed, or, if he had dreamed of it,
would have fancied himself the victim of some horrible nightmare.   I would not willingly lay myself
open to the imputation of applying this method to
Cervantes, and attribute to him a depth of intention
which, could he be asked about it, would call up in
his eyes the meditative smile that must habitually
have flickered there.   Spaniards have not been
wanting who protested against what they consider
to be the German fashion of interpreting their national author.   Don Juan Valera, in particular, one
of the best of contemporary Spanish men of letters,
both as critic and novelist, has argued the negative
side of the question with force and acumen in a
discourse pronounced on his admission to the Spanish Academy.   But I must confess that, while he
interested, he did not convince me.   I could quite
understand his impatience at what he considered
the supersubtleties of interpretation to which our
Teutonic cousins, who have taught us so much, are
certainly somewhat prone.   We have felt it ourselves when the obvious meaning of Shakespeare
has been rewritten into Hegelese, by some Doctor
of Philosophy desperate with the task of saying
something when everything had been already said,
and eager to apply his new theory of fog as an
illuminating medium.   But I do not think that
transcendental criticism can be charged with indis-
cretion in the case of " Don Quixote."   After reading all that can be said against the justice of its
deductions, or divinations if you choose to call
them so, I am inclined to say, as Turner did to the

lady who, after looking at one of his pictures, de-
clared that she could not see all this in nature,
" Madam, don't you wish to heaven you could ? "
I believe that in all really great imaginative work
we are aware, as in nature, of something far more
deeply interfused with our consciousness, under-
lying the obvious and familiar, as the living spirit
of them, and accessible only to a heightened sense
and a more passionate sympathy. He reads most
wisely who thinks everything into a book that
it is capable of holding, and it is the stamp and
token of a great book so to incorporate itself with
our own being, so to quicken our insight and stimulate our thought, as to make us feel as if we
helped to create it while we read. Whatever we
can find in a book that aids us in the conduct of
life, or to a truer interpretation of it, or to a franker
reconcilement with it, we may with a good conscience believe is not there by accident, but that
the author meant that we should find it there.
Cervantes certainly intended something of far
wider scope than a mere parody on the Romances
of Chivalry, which before his day had ceased to
have any vitality as motives of human conduct, or
even as pictures of a life that anybody believed to
have ever existed except in dreamland. That he
did intend his book as a good-humored criticism on
doctrinaire reformers who insist, in spite of all history and experience, on believing that society is
a device of human wit or an imposture of human
cunning, and not a growth, an evolution from natural causes, is clear enough in more than one pas-

sage to the thoughtful reader. It is also a satire
on all attempts to remake the world by the means
and methods of the past, and on the humanity of
impulse which looks on each fact that rouses its
pity or its sense of wrong as if it was or could be
complete in itself, and were not indissolubly bound
up with myriads of other facts both in the past
and the present. When we say that we are all of
us the result of the entire past, we perhaps are not
paying the past a very high compliment; but it is
no less true that whatever happens is in some
sense, more or less strict, the result of all that has
happened before. As with all men of heated im-
aginations, a near object of compassion occupies
the whole mind of Don Quixote; the figure of the
present sufferer looms gigantic and shuts out all
perception of remoter and more general considera-
tions. Don Quixote's quarrel is with the structure
of society, and it is only by degrees, through much
mistake and consequent suffering, that he finds out
how strong that structure is; nay, how strong it
must be in order that the world may go smoothly
and the course of events not be broken by a series
of cataclysms. The French Revolutionists with the
sincerest good intentions set about reforming in
Don Quixote's style, and France has been in com-
motion ever since. They carefully grubbed up
every root that drew its sustenance from the past,
and have been finding out ever since to their sorrow that nothing with roots can be made to order.
" Do right though the heavens fall " is an admirable precept so long as the heavens do not take you

at your word and come down about your ears —
still worse about those of your neighbors. It is a
rule rather of private than public obligation — for
indeed it is the doing of right that *keeps* the heavens from falling. After Don Quixote's temporary
rescue of the boy Andrés from his master's beating,
the manner in which he rides off and discharges his
mind of consequences is especially characteristic of
reform by theory without study of circumstances.
It is a profound stroke of humor that the reformer
Don Quixote should caution Sancho not to attempt
making the world over again, and to adapt himself
to things as he finds them.

In one of his adventures, it is in perfect keeping
that he should call on all the world to stop "till
he was satisfied." It is to be noted that in both
Don Quixote's attempts at the redress of particular
wrong (Andrés and the galley-slaves) the objects
(I might call them victims) of his benevolence
come back again to his discomfiture. In the case of
Andrés, Don Quixote can only blush, but Sancho
(the practical man without theories) gives the poor
fellow a hunch of bread and a few pennies, which
are very much to the purpose. Cervantes gives us
a plain hint here that all our mistakes sooner or
later surely come home to roost. It is remarkable how independent of time and circumstance the
satire of the great humorists always is. Aristoph-
anes, Rabelais, Shakespeare, Molière, seem to furnish side-lights to what we read in our morning
paper. As another instance of this in Cervantes,
who is continually illustrating it, read the whole

scene of the liberation of the galley-slaves. How
perfectly does it fit those humanitarians who cannot see the crime because the person of the criminal comes between them and it! That Cervantes
knew perfectly well what he was about in *his* satire
and saw beneath the surface of things is shown by
the apparition of the police and of the landlord
with the bill in his hand, for it was these that
brought the Good Old Times to their forlorn *Hic
Jacet.*

Coleridge, who in reach and range of intelligence, in penetration of insight, and in compre-
hensiveness of sympathy ranks among the first of
critics, says, "Don Quixote is not a man out of his
senses, but a man in whom the imagination and
the pure reason are so powerful as to make him
disregard the evidence of sense when it opposed
their conclusions. Sancho is the common sense of
the social man-animal unenlightened and unsanc-
tified by the reason. You see how he reverences
his master at the very time he is cheating him."
W. S. Landor thought that Coleridge took the hint
for this enlargement of the scope of the book from
him, but if I remember rightly it was Bouterwek
who first pointed criticism in the right direction.
Down to his time "Don Quixote" had been re-
garded as a burlesque, a farcical satire on the Romances of Chivalry, just as Shylock was so long
considered a character of low comedy.

But "Don Quixote," whatever its deeper meanings may be, has a literary importance almost
without parallel, and it is time that we should con-

sider it briefly. It would be hard to find a book more purely original and without precedent. Cervantes himself says in the preface to the First Part that he knows not what book he is following in it. Indeed, he follows none, though we find traces of his having read the "Golden Ass" and the Greek Romances. It was the first time that characters had been drawn from real life with such nicety and discrimination of touch, with such minuteness in particulars, and yet with such careful elimination of whatever was unessential that the personages are idealized to a proper artistic distance from mere actuality. With all this, how perfectly life-like they are! As Don Quixote tells us that he was almost ready to say he had seen Amadis, and proceeds to describe his personal appearance minutely, so we could affirm of the Knight of La Mancha and his Squire. They are real not because they are portraits, not because they are drawn from actual personages, but rather because of their very abstraction and generalization. They are not so much taken from life as informed with it. They are conceptions, not copies from any model; creations as no other characters but those of Shakespeare are in so full and adequate a manner; developed out of a seminal idea like the creatures of nature, not the matter-of-fact work of a detective's watchfulness, products of a quick eye and a faithful memory, but the true children of the imaginative faculty from which all the dregs of observation and memory have been distilled away, leaving only what is elementary and universal. I

confess that in the productions of what is called
the realistic school I too often find myself in company that is little to my taste, dragged back into
a commonplace world from which I was only too
glad to escape, and set to grind in the prison-
house of the Philistines. I walk about in a nightmare, the supreme horror of which is that my coat
is all buttonholes for bores to thrust their fingers
through and bait me to their heart's content.
Give me the writers who take me for a while out
of myself and (with pardon be it spoken) away
from my neighbors! I do not ask that characters
should be real; I need but go into the street to
find such in abundance. I ask only that they
should be possible, that they should be typical, because these I find in myself, and with these can
sympathize. Hector and Achilles, Clytemnestra
and Antigone, Roland and Oliver, Macbeth and
Lear, move about, if not in worlds not realized, at
least in worlds not realized to any eye but that of
imagination, a world far from the police reports, a
world into which it is a privilege, I might almost
call it an achievement, to enter. Don Quixote and
his Squire are inhabitants of this world, in spite of
the prosaic and often vulgar stage on which their
tragi-comedy is acted, because they are symbolical,
because they represent the two great factors of
human character and springs of human action —
the Imagination and the Understanding. If you
would convince yourself how true this is, compare
them with Sir Hudibras and Ralpho — or still
better with Roderick Random and Strap. There

can be no better proof that Cervantes meant to contrast the ideal with the matter of fact in the two characters than his setting side by side images of the same woman as reflected in the eyes of Sancho and of his master; in other words, as seen by common-sense and by passion.[1]

I shall not trouble you with any labored analysis of humor. If you wish to know what humor is, I should say read "Don Quixote." It is the element in which the whole story lives and moves and has its being, and it wakens and flashes round the course of the narrative like a phosphorescent sea in the track of a ship. It is nowhere absent; it is nowhere obtrusive; it lightens and plays about the surface for a moment and is gone. It is everywhere by suggestion, it is nowhere with emphasis and insistence. There is infinite variety, yet always in harmony with the characters and the purpose of the fable. The impression it produces is cumulative, not sudden or startling. It is unobtrusive as the tone of good conversation. I am not speaking of the *fun* of the book, of which there is plenty, and sometimes boisterous enough, but of that deeper and more delicate quality, suggestive of remote analogies and essential incongruities, which alone deserves the name of humor.

This quality is so diffused in "Don Quixote," so thoroughly permeates every pore and fibre of the book, that it is difficult to exemplify it by citation. Take as examples the scene with the goatherds, where Don Quixote, after having amply supped,

[1] Part. Prim. cap. x., xxxi.

discourses so eloquently of that Golden Age which was happy in having nothing to eat but acorns or to drink but water; where, while insisting that Sancho should assume equality as a man, he denies it to him as Sancho, by reminding him that it is granted by one who is his natural lord and master, — there is such a difference, alas, between universal and particular Brotherhood! Take the debate of Don Quixote (already mad) as to what form of madness he should assume; the quarrel of the two madmen, Don Quixote and Cardénio, about the good fame of Queen Madásima, a purely imaginary being; the resolution of Don Quixote, when forced to renounce knight-errantry, that he will become a shepherd of the kind known to poets, thus exchanging one unreality for another. Nay, take the whole book, if you would learn what humor is, whether in its most obvious or its most subtle manifestations. The highest and most complete illustration is the principal character of the story. I do not believe that a character so absolutely perfect in conception and delineation, so psychologically true, so full of whimsical inconsistencies, all combining to produce an impression of perfect coherence, is to be found in fiction. He was a monomaniac,[1] all of whose faculties, his very senses themselves, are subjected by one overmastering prepossession, and at last conspire with it, almost against their will, in spite of daily disillusion and of the uniform testimony of facts and

[1] That Cervantes had made a study of madness is evident from the Introduction to the Second Part.

events to the contrary. The key to Don Quixote's character is given in the first chapter where he is piecing out his imperfect helmet with a new visor. He makes one of pasteboard, and then, testing it with his sword, shatters it to pieces. He proceeds to make another strengthened with strips of iron, and "without caring to make a further trial of it, commissioned and held it for the finest possible visor." Don Quixote always sees what he wishes to see, and yet always sees things as they are unless the necessities of his hallucination compel him to see them otherwise, and it is wonderful with what ingenuity he makes everything bend to those necessities. Cervantes calls him the sanest madman and the maddest reasonable man in the world. Sancho says that he was fitter to be preacher than knight-errant. He *makes* facts curtsy to his prepossessions. At the same time, with exact truth to nature, he is never perfectly convinced himself except in moments of exaltation, and when the bee in his bonnet buzzes so loudly as to prevent his hearing the voice of reason. Cervantes takes care to tell us that he was never convinced that he was really a knight-errant till his ceremonious reception at the castle of the Duke.

Sancho, on the other hand, sees everything in the dry light of common sense, except when beguiled by cupidity or under the immediate spell of his master's imagination. Grant the imagination its premises, and its logic is irresistible. Don Quixote always takes these premises for granted, and Sancho, despite his natural shrewdness, is more than half tempted to admit them, or at any rate to run the risk of their being sound, partly out of habitual respect for his master's superior rank and knowledge, partly on the chance of the reward which his master perpetually dangled before him. This reward was that island of which Don Quixote confesses he cannot tell the name because it is not down on any map.   With delightful humor, it begins as *some* island, then becomes *the* island, and then one of those islands.   And how much more probable does this vagueness render the fulfilment of the promise than if Don Quixote had locked himself up in a specific *one!*   A line of retreat is thus always kept open, while Sancho's eagerness is held at bay by this seemingly chance suggestion of a choice in these hypothetical lordships.   This vague potentiality of islands eludes the thrust of any definite objection.   And when Sancho is inclined to grumble, his master consoles him by saying, " I have already told thee, Sancho, to give thyself no care about it ; for even should the island fail us, there are the kingdoms of Dinamarca and Sobradisa that would fit you as the ring fits the finger, and since they are on *terra firma,* you should rejoice the more."   As if these were more easily to be come at, though all his *terra firma* was in dreamland too.   It should seem that Sancho was too shrewd for such a bait, and that here at least was an exception to that probability for which I have praised the story.   But I think it rather a justification of it.   We must remember how near the epoch of the story was to that of the *Con-*

quistadores, when men's fancies were still glowing with the splendid potentialities of adventure. And when Don Quixote suggests the possibility of creating Sancho a marquis, it is remarkable that he mentions the title conferred upon Cortés. The conscience of Don Quixote is in loyalty to his ideal; he prizes desert as an inalienable possession of the soul. The conscience of Sancho is in the eyes of his neighbors, and he values repute for its worldly advantages. When Sancho tries to divert his master from the adventure of the Fulling Mills by arguing that it was night, and that none could see them, so that they might well turn out of the way to avoid the danger, and begs him rather to take a little sleep, Don Quixote answers indignantly: "Sleep thou, who wast born for sleep. As for me, I shall do whatever I see to be most becoming to my profession." With equal truth to nature in both cases, Sancho is represented as inclined to believe the extravagant delusions of his master because he has seen and known him all his life, while he obstinately refuses to believe that a barber's basin is the helmet of Mambrino because he sees and knows that it is a basin. Don Quixote says of him to the Duke, "He doubts everything and believes everything." Cervantes was too great an artist to make him wholly vulgar and greedy and selfish, though he makes him all these. He is witty, wise according to his lights, affectionate, and faithful. When he takes leave of his imaginary governorship he is not without a certain manly dignity that is almost pathetic.

The ingenuity of the story, the probability of its adventures, the unwearied fecundity of invention shown in devising and interlacing them, in giving variety to a single theme and to a plot so perfectly simple in its conception, are all wonderful. The narrative flows on as if unconsciously, and our fancies are floated along upon it. It is noticeable, too, in passing, what a hypæthral story it is, how much of it passes in the open air, how the sun shines, the birds sing, the brooks dance, and the leaves murmur in it. This is peculiarly touching when we recollect that it was written in prison. In the First Part Cervantes made the mistake (as he himself afterwards practically admits) of introducing unprofitable digressions, and in respect to the propriety and congruousness of the adventures which befall Don Quixote I must also make one exception. I mean the practical jokes played upon him at the Duke's castle, in which his delusion is forced upon him instead of adapting circumstances to itself or itself to circumstances, according to the necessity of the occasion. These tend to degrade him in the eyes of the reader, who resents rather than enjoys them, and feels the essential vulgarity of his tormentors through all their fine clothes. It is quite otherwise with the cheats put upon Sancho, for we feel that either he will be shrewd enough to be more than even with the framers of them, or that he is of too coarse a fibre to feel them keenly. But Don Quixote is a gentleman and a monomaniac,— qualities, the one of which renders such rudeness incongruous, and the other unfeeling. He is, moreover, a guest. It is curious that Shakespeare makes the same mistake with Falstaff in the "Merry Wives of Windsor," and Fielding with Parson Adams, and in both cases to our discomfort. The late Mr. Edward Fitzgerald (*quis desiderio sit pudor aut modus tam cari capitis!*) preferred the Second Part to the First, and, but for these scenes, which always pain and anger me, I should agree with him. For it is plain that Cervantes became slowly conscious as he went on how rich was the vein he had hit upon, how full of various and profound suggestion were the two characters he had conceived and who together make a complete man. No doubt he at first proposed to himself a parody of the Romances of Chivalry, but his genius soon broke away from the leading-strings of a plot that denied free scope to his deeper conception of life and men.

Cervantes is the father of the modern novel, in so far as it has become a study and delineation of character instead of being a narrative seeking to interest by situation and incident. He has also more or less directly given impulse and direction to all humoristic literature since his time. We see traces of him in Molière, in Swift, and still more clearly in Sterne and Richter. Fielding assimilated and Smollett copied him. Scott was his disciple in the "Antiquary," that most delightful of his delightful novels. Irving imitated him in his "Knickerbocker," and Dickens in his "Pickwick Papers." I do not mention this as detracting from *their* originality, but only as showing the wonderful

virility of *his*.   The pedigrees of books are as interesting and instructive as those of men.   It is
also good for us to remember that this man whose
life was outwardly a failure restored to Spain the
universal empire she had lost.

HARVARD ANNIVERSARY

ADDRESS DELIVERED IN SANDERS THEATRE, CAM-
BRIDGE, NOVEMBER 8, 1886, ON THE TWO HUNDRED
AND FIFTIETH ANNIVERSARY OF THE FOUNDATION OF
HARVARD UNIVERSITY.

IT seems an odd anomaly that, while respect for
age and deference to its opinions have diminished
and are still sensibly diminishing among us, the
relish of antiquity should be more pungent and
the value set upon things merely because they are
old should be greater in America than anywhere
else. It is merely a sentimental relish, for ours is
a new country in more senses than one, and, like
children when they are fancying themselves this or
that, we have to play very hard in order to believe
that we are old. But we like the game none the
worse, and multiply our anniversaries with honest
zeal, as if we increased our centuries by the number of events we could congratulate on having happened a hundred years ago. There is something
of instinct in this, and it is a wholesome instinct if
it serve to quicken our consciousness of the forces
that are gathered by duration and continuity; if
it teach us that, ride fast and far as we may, we
carry the Past on our crupper, as immovably seated
there as the black Care of the Roman poet. The

generations of men are braided inextricably together, and the very trick of our gait may be countless generations older than we.

I have sometimes wondered whether, as the faith
of men in a future existence grew less confident,
they might not be seeking some equivalent in the
feeling of a retrospective duration, if not their
own, at least that of their race. Yet even this con-
tinuance is trifling and ephemeral. If the tablets
unearthed and deciphered by Geology have forced
us to push back incalculably the birthday of man,
they have in like proportion impoverished his recorded annals, making even the Platonic year but
as a single grain of the sand in Time's hour-glass,
and the inscriptions of Egypt and Assyria modern
as yesterday's newspaper. Fancy flutters over
these vague wastes like a butterfly blown out to
sea, and finds no foothold. It is true that, if we
may put as much faith in heredity as seems reasonable to many of us, we are all in some transcendental sense the coevals of primitive man, and
Pythagoras may well have been present in Euphor-
bus at the siege of Troy. Had Shakespeare's
thought taken this turn when he said to Time —

> " Thy pyramids built up with newer might
> To me are nothing novel, nothing strange ;
> They are but dressings of a former sight " ?

But this imputed and vicarious longevity, though
it may be obscurely operative in our lives and fortunes, is no valid offset for the shortness of our
days, nor widens by a hair's breadth the horizon of
our memories. Man and his monuments are of

yesterday, and we, however we may play with our fancies, must content ourselves with being young. If youth be a defect, it is one that we outgrow only too soon.

Mr. Ruskin said the other day that he could not live in a country that had neither castles nor cathedrals, and doubtless men of imaginative temper find not only charm but inspiration in structures which Nature has adopted as her foster-children, and on which Time has laid his hand only in benediction. It is not their antiquity, but its association with man, that endows them with such sensitizing potency. Even the landscape sometimes bewitches us by this glamour of a human past, and the green pastures and golden slopes of England are sweeter both to the outward and to the inward eye that the hand of man has immemorially cared for and caressed them. The nightingale sings with more prevailing passion in Greece that we first heard her from the thickets of a Euripidean chorus. For myself, I never felt the working of this spell so acutely as in those gray seclusions of the college quadrangles and cloisters at Oxford and Cambridge, conscious with venerable associations, and whose very stones seemed happier for being there. The chapel pavement still whispered with the blessed feet of that long procession of saints and sages and scholars and poets, who are all gone into a world of light, but whose memories seem to consecrate the soul from all ignobler companionship.

Are we to suppose that these memories were less dear and gracious to the Puritan scholars, at whose instigation this college was founded, than to that other Puritan who sang the dim religious light, the long-drawn aisles and fretted vaults, which these memories recalled? Doubtless all these things were present to their minds, but they were ready to forego them all for the sake of that truth whereof, as Milton says of himself, they were members incorporate. The pitiful contrast which they must have felt between the carven sanctuaries of learning they had left behind and the wattled fold they were rearing here on the edge of the wilderness is to me more than tenderly — it is almost sublimely — pathetic. When I think of their unpliable strength of purpose, their fidelity to their ideal, their faith in God and in themselves, I am inclined to say with Donne that

" We are scarce our fathers' shadows cast at noon."

Our past is well-nigh desolate of æsthetic stimulus. We have none or next to none of these aids to the imagination, of these coigns of vantage for the tendrils of memory or affection. Not one of our older buildings is venerable, or will ever become so. Time refuses to console them. They all look as if they meant business, and nothing more. And it is precisely because this College meant business, business of the gravest import, and did that business as thoroughly as it might with no means that were not niggardly except an abundant purpose to do its best, — it is precisely for this that we have gathered here to-day. We come back hither from the experiences of a richer life, as the son who has prospered returns to the household of his youth, to find in its very homeliness a pulse, if not of deeper, certainly of fonder, emotion than any splendor could stir. " Dear old Mother," we say, " how charming you are in your plain cap and the drab silk that has been turned again since we saw you ! You were constantly forced to remind us that you could not afford to give us this and that which some other boys had, but your discipline and diet were wholesome, and you sent us forth into the world with the sound constitutions and healthy appetites that are bred of simple fare."

It is good for us to commemorate this homespun past of ours ; good, in these days of a reckless and swaggering prosperity, to remind ourselves how poor our fathers were, and that we celebrate them because for themselves and their children they chose wisdom and understanding and the things that are of God rather than any other riches. This is our Founders' Day, and we are come together to do honor to them all : first, to the Commonwealth which laid our corner-stone ; next, to the gentle and godly youth from whom we took our name, — himself scarce more than a name, — and with them to the countless throng of benefactors, rich and poor, who have built us up to what we are. We cannot do it better than in the familiar words : " Let us now praise famous men and our fathers that begat us. The Lord hath wrought great glory by them through his great power from the beginning. Leaders of the people by their counsels, and, by their knowledge of learning, meet for the people ; wise and eloquent in their instructions. There be of them that have left a name behind them that their praises might be reported. And some there be which have no memorial, who are perished as though they had never been. But these were merciful men whose righteousness hath not been forgotten. With their seed shall continually remain a good inheritance. Their seed standeth fast, and their children for their sakes."

This two hundred and fiftieth anniversary of our College is not remarkable as commemorating any memorable length of days. There is hardly a country in Europe but can show us universities that were older than ours now is when ours was but a grammar-school, with Eaton as master. Bologna, Paris, Oxford, were already famous schools when Dante visited them, as I love to think he did, six hundred years ago. We are ancient, it is true, on our own continent, ancient even as compared with several German universities more renowned than we. But it is not primarily the longevity of our Alma Mater upon which we are gathered here to congratulate her and each other. Kant says somewhere that, as the records of human transactions accumulate, the memory of man will have room only for those of supreme cosmopolitical importance. Can we claim for the birthday we are keeping a significance of so wide a bearing and so long a reach? If we may not do that, we may at least affirm confidently that the event it records and emphasizes is second in real import to none that has happened in this western hemisphere.

The material growth of the colonies would have brought about their political separation from the Mother Country in the fulness of time, without that stain of blood which unhappily keeps its own memory green so long. But the founding of the first English college here was what saved New England from becoming a mere geographical expression. It did more, for it insured, and I believe was meant to insure, our intellectual independence of the Old World. That independence has been long in coming, but it will come at last; and are not the names of the chiefest of those who have hastened its coming written on the roll of Harvard College?

I think this foundation of ours a quite unexampled thing. Surely never were the bases of such a structure as this has become, and was meant to be, laid by a community of men so poor, in circumstances so unprecedented, and under what seemed such sullen and averted stars. The colony, still insignificant, was in danger of an Indian war, was in the throes of that Antinomian controversy which threatened its very existence, yet the leaders of opinion on both sides were united in the resolve that sound learning and an educated clergy should never cease from among them or their descendants in the commonwealth they were building up. In the midst of such fears and such tumults Harvard College was born, and not Marina herself had a more blusterous birth or a more chiding nativity. The prevision of those men must have been as clear as their faith was steadfast. Well they knew and had laid to heart the wise man's precept, "Take fast hold of instruction; let her not go; for she is thy life."

There can be little question that the action of the General Court received its impulse and direction from the clergy, men of eminent qualities and of well-deserved authority. Among the Massachusetts Bay colonists the proportion of ministers, trained at Oxford and Cambridge, was surprisingly large, and, if we may trust the evidence of contemporary secular literature, such men as Higginson, Cotton, Wilson, Norton, Shepard, Bulkley, Davenport, to mention no more, were, in learning, intelligence, and general accomplishment, far above the average parson of the country and the church from which their consciences had driven them out. The presence and influence of such men were of inestimable consequence to the fortunes of the colony. If they were narrow, it was as the Sword of Righteousness is narrow. If they had but one idea, it was as the leader of a forlorn hope has but one, and can have no other, namely, to do the duty that is laid on him, and ask no questions. Our Puritan ancestors have been misrepresented and maligned by persons without imagination enough to make themselves contemporary with, and therefore able to understand, the men whose memories they strive to blacken. That happy breed of men who, both in church and state, led our first emigration, were children of the most splendid intellectual epoch that England has ever known. They were the coevals of a generation which passed on in scarcely

diminished radiance the torch of life kindled in
great Eliza's golden days.   Out of the New Learning, the new ferment alike religious and national,
and the New Discoveries with their suggestion
of boundless possibility, the alembic of that age
had distilled a potent elixir either inspiring or
intoxicating, as the mind that imbibed it was
strong or weak.   Are we to suppose that the lips
of the founders of New England alone were un-
wetted by a drop of that stimulating draught? —
that Milton was the only Puritan that had read
Shakespeare and Ben Jonson and Beaumont and
Fletcher?   I do not believe it, whoever may.   Did
they flee from persecution to become themselves
persecutors in turn?   This means only that they
would not permit their holy enterprise to be hindered or their property to be damaged even by men
with the most pious intentions and as sincere, if not
always so wise, as they.   They would not stand any
nonsense, as the phrase is, a mood of mind from
which their descendants seem somewhat to have
degenerated.   They were no more unreasonable
than the landlady of Taylor the Platonist in refusing to let him sacrifice a bull to Jupiter in her
back-parlor.   The New England Puritans of the
second generation became narrow enough, and pup-
pets of that formalism against which their fathers
had revolted.   But this was the inevitable result
of that isolation which cut them off from the great
currents of cosmopolitan thought and action.   Communities as well as men have a right to be judged
by their best.   We are justified in taking the elder

Winthrop as a type of the leading emigrants, and
the more we know him the more we learn to reverence his great qualities, whether of mind or character.   The posterity of those earnest and single-
minded men may have thrown the creed of their
fathers into the waste-basket, but their fidelity to it
and to the duties they believed it to involve is the
most precious and potent drop in their transmitted
blood.   It is especially noteworthy that they did not
make a strait-waistcoat of this creed for their new
college.   The more I meditate upon them, the more
I am inclined to pardon the enthusiasm of our old
preacher when he said that God had sifted three
kingdoms to plant New England.[1]

The Massachusetts Bay Colony itself also was
then and since without a parallel.   It was established by a commercial company, whose members
combined in themselves the two by no means incongruous elements of religious enthusiasm and business sagacity, the earthy ingredient, as in dyna-
mite, holding in check its explosive partner, which
yet could and did explode on sufficient concussion.
They meant that their venture should be gainful,
but at the same time believed that nothing could
be long profitable for the body wherein the soul
found not also her advantage.   They feared God,

---

[1] Writing in the country, with almost no books about me, I
have been obliged to trust wholly to my memory in my references.
My friend Dr. Charles Deane, the most learned of our historical
antiquarians, kindly informs me that the passage alluded to in
the text should read, " God sifted a whole Nation that he might
send choice Grain out into this Wilderness." Stoughton's Election Sermon, preached in 1668.

and kept their powder dry because they feared Him and meant that others should. I think their most remarkable characteristic was their public spirit, and in nothing did they show both that and the wise forecast that gives it its best value more clearly than when they resolved to keep the higher education of youth in their own hands and under their own eye. This they provided for in the College. Eleven years later they established their system of public schools, where reading and writing should be taught. This they did partly, no doubt, to provide feeders for the more advanced schools, and so for the College, but even more, it may safely be inferred, because they had found that the polity to which their ends, rough-hew them as they might, must be shaped, by the conditions under which they were forced to act, could be safe only in the hands of intelligent men, or, at worst, of men to whom they had given a chance to become such.

In founding the College, they had three objects: first, the teaching of the Humanities and of Hebrew, as the hieratic language; second, the training of a learned as well as godly clergy; and third, the education of the Indians, that they might serve as missionaries of a higher civilization and of a purer religion, as the necessary preliminary thereto. The third of these objects, after much effort and much tribulation, they were forced to abandon. John Winthrop, Jr., in a letter written to the Honorable Robert Boyle in 1663, gives us an interesting glimpse of a pair of these dusky catechumens. " I make bold," he says, " to send heere inclosed a kind of rarity ; . . . It is two papers of Latin composed by two Indians now scollars in the Colledge in this country, and the writing is with their own hands. . . . Possibly as a novelty of that kind it may be acceptable, being a reall fruit of that hopefull worke y^t is begū amongst them . . . testifying thus much that I received them of those Indians out of their own hands, and had ready answers frō them in Latin to many questions that I propounded to them in y^t language, and heard them both express severall sentences in Greke also. I doubt not but those honorable *fautores Scientiarum* [the Royal Society] will gladly receive the intelligence of such *Vestigia Doctrinœ* in this wilderness amongst such a barbarous people." Alas, these *Vestigia* became only too soon *retrorsum !* The Indians showed a far greater natural predisposition for disfurnishing the outside of other people's heads than for furnishing the insides of their own. Their own wild life must have been dear to them; the forest beckoned just outside the College door, and the first blue-bird of spring whistled them back to the woods. They would have said to the president, with the Gypsy steward in the old play when he heard the new-come nightingale, " Oh, Sir, you hear I am called." At any rate, our College succeeded in keeping but one of these wild creatures long enough to make a graduate of him, and he thereupon vanishes into the merciful shadow of the past. His name — but, as there was only one Indian graduate, so there is only one living man who can pronounce his unconverted name, and I leave the task to Dr. Hammond Trumbull.

I shall not attempt, even in brief, a history of the College. It has already been excellently done. A compendium of it would be mainly a list of unfamiliar names, and Coleridge has said truly that such names " are non-conductors ; they stop all interest."

The fame and usefulness of all institutions of learning depend on the greatness of those who teach in them,

" Queis arte benigna,
Et meliore luto finxit præcordia Titan,"

and great teachers are almost rarer than great poets. We can lay claim to none such (I must not speak of the living), unless it be Agassiz, whom we adopted, but we have had many devoted and some eminent. It has not been their fault if they have not pushed farther forward the boundaries of knowledge. Our professors have been compelled by the necessities of the case (as we are apt to call things which we ought to reform, but do not) to do too much work not properly theirs, and that of a kind so exacting as to consume the energy that might have been ample for higher service. They have been obliged to double the parts of professor and tutor. They have been underpaid and the balance made good to them by being overworked. During the seventeenth century we have reason to think that the College kept pretty well up to the standard of its contemporary colleges in England, so far as its poverty would allow. It seems to have enjoyed a certain fame abroad among men who sympathized with the theology it taught, for I possess a Hebrew Accidence, dedicated some two hundred years ago to the " illustrious academy at Boston in New England," by a Dutch scholar whom I cannot help thinking a very discerning person. That the students of that day had access to a fairly good library may be inferred from Cotton Mather's " Magnalia," though he knew not how to make the best use of it, and is a very nightmare of pedantry. That the College had made New England a good market for books is proved by John Dunton's journey hither in the interests of his trade. During the eighteenth and first quarter of the nineteenth centuries, I fancy the condition of things here to have been very much what it was in the smaller English colleges of the period, if we may trust the verses which Gray addressed to the goddess Ignorance. Young men who were willing mainly to teach themselves might get something to their advantage, while the rest were put here by their parents as into a comfortable quarantine, where they could wait till the gates of life were opened to them, safe from any contagion of learning, except such as might be developed from previous infection. I am speaking of a great while ago. Men are apt, I know, in after life to lay the blame of their scholastic shortcomings at the door of their teachers. They are often wrong in this, and I am quite aware that there are some pupils who are knowledge-proof; but I gather from tradition, which I believe to be trust-

worthy, that there have been periods in the history
of the College when the students might have sung
with Bishop Golias : —

> " Hi nos docent, sed indocti ;
> Hi nos docent, et nox nocti
> Indicat scientiam."

Despite all this, it is remarkable that the two
first American imaginative artists, Allston in painting and Greenough in sculpture, were graduates of
Harvard. A later generation is justly proud of
Story.

We have a means of testing the general culture
given here towards the middle of the last century
in the *Gratulatio* presented by Harvard College
on the accession of George III. It is not duller
than such things usually are on the other side of
the water, and it shows a pretty knack at tagging
verses. It is noteworthy that the Greek in it, if I
remember rightly, is wholly or chiefly Governor
Bernard's. A few years earlier, some of the tracts
in the Whitfield controversy prove that the writers
had got here a thorough training in English at
least. They had certainly not read their Swift in
vain.

But the chief service, as it was the chief office,
of the College during all those years was to maintain and hand down the traditions of how excellent
a thing Learning was, even if the teaching were
not always adequate by way of illustration. And
yet, so far as that teaching went, it was wise in
this, that it gave its pupils some tincture of letters
as distinguished from mere scholarship. It aimed

to teach them the authors, that is, the few great
ones, — the late Professor Popkin, whom the older
of us remember, would have allowed that title only
to the Greeks, — and to teach them in such a way
as to enable the pupil to assimilate somewhat of
their thought, sentiment, and style, rather than to
master the minuter niceties of the language in
which they wrote. It struck for their matter, as
Montaigne advised, who would have men taught to
love Virtue instead of learning to decline *virtus*.
It set more store by the marrow than by the bone
that encased it. It made language, as it should be,
a ladder to literature, and not literature a ladder
to language. Many a boy has hated, and rightly
hated, Homer and Horace the pedagogues and
grammarians, who would have loved Homer and
Horace the poets, had he been allowed to make
their acquaintance. The old method of instruction
had the prime merit of enabling its pupils to conceive that there is neither ancient nor modern on
the narrow shelves of what is truly literature. We
owe a great debt to the Germans. No one is more
indebted to them than I, but is there not danger of
their misleading us in some directions into pedantry? In his preface to an Old French poem of the
thirteenth century, lately published, the editor informs us sorrowfully that he had the advantage of
listening only two years and a half to the lectures
of Professor Gaston Paris, in which time he got
no farther than through the first three vowels. At
this rate, to master the whole alphabet, consonants
and all, would be a task fitter for the centurial ado-

lescence of Methuselah than for our less liberal ration of years. I was glad my editor had had this
advantage under so competent a master, and I am
quite willing that Old French should get the benefit of such scrupulosity, but I think I see a tendency to train young men in the languages as if
they were all to be editors, and not lovers of polite
literature. Education, we are often told, is a drawing out of the faculties. May they not be drawn
out too thin? I am not undervaluing philology or
accuracy of scholarship. Both are excellent and
admirable in their places. But philology is less
beautiful to me than philosophy, as Milton understood the word, and mere accuracy is to Truth as a
plaster-cast to the marble statue ; it gives the facts,
but not their meaning. If I must choose, I had
rather a young man should be intimate with the
genius of the Greek dramatic poets than with the
metres of their choruses, though I should be glad
to have him on easy terms with both.

For more than two hundred years, in its discipline and courses of study, the College followed
mainly the lines traced by its founders. The influence of its first half century did more than any
other, perhaps more than all others, to make New
England what it is. During the one hundred and
forty years preceding our War of Independence it
had supplied the schools of the greater part of New
England with teachers. What was even more important, it had sent to every parish in Massachusetts one man, the clergyman, with a certain amount
of scholarship, a belief in culture, and generally

pretty sure to bring with him or to gather a considerable collection of books, by no means wholly
theological. Simple and godly men were they, the
truest modern antitypes of Chaucer's Good Parson,
receiving much, sometimes all, of their scanty sal-
ary in kind, and eking it out by the drudgery of a
cross-grained farm where the soil seems all back-
bone. If there was no regular practitioner, they
practised without fee a grandmotherly sort of medi-
cine, probably not much more harmful (*O, dura
messorum ilia*) than the heroic treatment of the
day. They contrived to save enough to send their
sons through college, to portion their daughters,
decently trained in English literature of the more
serious kind, and perfect in the duties of household
and dairy, and to make modest provision for the
widow, if they should leave one. With all this,
they gave their two sermons every Sunday of the
year, and of a measure that would seem ruinously
liberal to these less stalwart days, when scarce ten
parsons together could lift the stones of Diomed
which they hurled at Satan with the easy precision
of lifelong practice. And if they turned their bar-
rel of discourses at the end of the Horatian ninth
year, which of their parishioners was the wiser for
it? Their one great holiday was Commencement,
which they punctually attended. They shared the
many toils and the rare festivals, the joys and the
sorrows, of their townsmen as bone of their bone
and flesh of their flesh, for all were of one blood
and of one faith. They dwelt on the same bro-
therly level with them as men, yet set apart from

and above them by their sacred office. Preaching the most terrible of doctrines, as most of them did, they were humane and cheerful men, and when they came down from the pulpit seemed to have been merely twisting their " cast-iron logic " of despair, as Coleridge said of Donne, " into true-love-knots." Men of authority, wise in council, independent, for their settlement was a life-tenure, they were living lessons of piety, industry, frugality, temperance, and, with the magistrates, were a recognized aristocracy. Surely never was an aristocracy so simple, so harmless, so exemplary, and so fit to rule. I remember a few lingering survivors of them in my early boyhood, relics of a serious but not sullen past, of a community for which in civic virtue, intelligence, and general efficacy I seek a parallel in vain : —

> " rusticorum mascula militum
> Proles . . . docta . . .
>   Versare glebas et severæ
> Matris ad arbitrium recisos
>   Portare fustes."

I know too well the deductions to be made. It was a community without charm, or with a homely charm at best, and the life it led was visited by no muse even in dream. But it was the stuff out of which fortunate ancestors are made, and twenty-five years ago their sons showed in no diminished measure the qualities of the breed. In every household some brave boy was saying to his mother, as Iphigenia to hers, —

Πᾶσι γάρ μ᾿ Ἕλλησι κοινὸν ἔτεκες οὐχὶ σοὶ μόνῃ.

Nor were Harvard's sons the last. This hall commemorates them, but their story is written in headstones all over the land they saved.

To the teaching and example of those reverend men whom Harvard bred and then planted in every hamlet as pioneers and outposts of her doctrine, Massachusetts owes the better part of her moral and intellectual inheritance. They, too, were the progenitors of a numerous and valid race. My friend Dr. Holmes was, I believe, the first to point out how large a proportion of our men of light and leading sprang from their loins. The illustrious Chief Magistrate of the Republic, who honors us with his presence here to-day, has ancestors italicized in our printed registers, and has shown himself worthy of his pedigree.

During the present century, I believe that Harvard received and welcomed the new learning from Germany at the hands of Everett, Bancroft, and Ticknor, before it had been accepted by the more conservative universities of the Old Home. Everett's translation of Buttmann's Greek Grammar was reprinted in England, with the " Massachusetts " omitted after " Cambridge," at the end of the preface, to conceal its American origin. Emerson has told us how his intellectual life was quickened by the eloquent enthusiasm of Everett's teaching. Mr. Bancroft made strenuous efforts to introduce a more wholesome discipline and maturer methods of study, with the result of a rebellion of the Freshman Class, who issued a manifesto of their wrongs, written by the late Robert Rantoul, which ended thus: "Shall FREEMEN bear this? FRESHMEN are freemen!" They, too, remembered Revolutionary sires. Mr. Bancroft's translation of Heeren was the first of its kind, and it is worth mention that the earliest version from the prose of Heinrich Heine into English was made here, though not by a graduate of Harvard. Ticknor also strove earnestly to enlarge the scope of the collegiate courses of study. The force of the new impulse did not last long, or produce, unless indirectly, lasting results. It was premature, the students were really school-boys, and the College was not yet capable of the larger university life. The conditions of American life, too, were such that young men looked upon scholarship neither as an end nor as a means, but simply as an accomplishment, like music or dancing, of which they were to acquire a little more or a little less, generally a little less, according to individual taste or circumstances. It has been mainly during the last twenty-five years that the College, having already the name, but by no means all the resources, of a university, has been trying to perform some, at least, of the functions which that title implies.

> "Now half appears
> The tawny lion, pawing to get free."

Let us, then, no longer look backwards, but forwards, as our fathers did when they laid our humble foundations in the wilderness. The motto first proposed for the College arms was, as you know, *Veritas*, written across three open books. It was a noble one, and, if the full bearing of it was understood, as daring as it was noble. Perhaps it was discarded because an *open* book seemed hardly the fittest symbol for what is so hard to find, and, if ever we fancy we have found it, so hard to decipher and to translate into our own language and life. Pilate's question still murmurs in the ear of every thoughtful, and Montaigne's in that of every honest man. The motto finally substituted for that, *Christo et Ecclesiæ*, is, when rightly interpreted, substantially the same, for it means that we are to devote ourselves to the highest conception we have of Truth and to the preaching of it. Fortunately, the Sphinx proposes her conundrums to us one at a time and at intervals proportioned to our wits.

Joseph de Maistre says that "un homme d'esprit est tenu de savoir deux choses : 1°, ce qu'il est ; 2°, où il est." The questions for us are, In what sense and how far are we become a university? And then, if we fully become so, What and to what end should a university aim to teach now and here in this America of ours whose meaning no man can yet comprehend? And, when we have settled what it is best to teach, comes the further question, How are we to teach it? Whether with an eye to its effect on developing character or personal availability, that is to say, to its effect in the conduct of life, or on the chances of getting a livelihood? Perhaps we shall find that we must have a care for both, and I cannot see why the two need be incompatible ; but if they are, I should choose the former term of the alternative.

In a not remote past, society had still certain

recognized, authoritative guides, and the College trained them as the fashion of the day required. But

" Damnosa quid non imminuit dies ? "

That ancient close corporation of official guides has been compelled to surrender its charter. We are pestered with as many volunteers as at Niagara, and, as there, if we follow any of them, may count on paying for it pretty dearly. The office of the higher instruction, nevertheless, continues to be as it always was, the training of such guides; only it must now try to fit them out with as much more personal accomplishment and authority as may compensate the loss of hierarchical prestige.

When President Walker, it must be now nearly thirty years ago, asked me in common with my colleagues what my notion of a university was, I answered, " A university is a place where nothing useful is taught; but a university is possible only where a man may get his livelihood by digging Sanscrit roots." What I meant was that the highest office of the somewhat complex thing so named was to distribute the true Bread of Life, the *pane 'degli angeli,* as · Dante called it, and to breed an appetite for it; but that it should also have the means and appliances for teaching everything, as the mediæval universities aimed to do in their *trivium* and *quadrivium.* I had in mind the ideal and the practical sides of the institution, and was thinking also whether such an institution was practicable, and, if so, whether it was desirable, in a country like this. I think it eminently desirable, and, if it be, what should be its chief function? I choose rather to hesitate my opinion than to assert it roundly. But some opinion I am bound to have, either my own or another man's, if I would be in the fashion, though I may not be wholly satisfied with the one or the other. Opinions are "as handy," to borrow our Yankee proverb, "as a pocket in a shirt," and, I may add, as hard to come at. I hope, then, that the day will come when a competent professor may lecture here also for three years on the first three vowels of the Romance alphabet, and find fit audience, though few. I hope the day may never come when the weightier matters of a language, namely, such parts of its literature as have overcome death by reason of their wisdom and of the beauty in which it is incarnated, such parts as are universal by reason of their civilizing properties, their power to elevate and fortify the mind, — I hope the day may never come when these are not predominant in the teaching given here. Let the Humanities be maintained undiminished in their ancient right. Leave in their traditional preëminence those arts that were rightly called liberal; those studies that kindle the imagination, and through it irradiate the reason; those studies that manumitted the modern mind; those in which the brains of finest temper have found alike their stimulus and their repose, taught by them that the power of intellect is heightened in proportion as it is made gracious by measure and symmetry. Give us science, too, but give first of all, and last of all, the science that ennobles life and makes it generous. I stand here as a man of letters, and as a man of letters I must speak. But I am speaking with no exclusive intention. No one believes more firmly than I in the usefulness, I might well say the necessity, of variety in study, and of opening the freest scope possible to the prevailing bent of every mind when that bent shows itself to be so predominating as to warrant it. Many-sidedness of culture makes our vision clearer and keener in particulars. For after all, the noblest definition of Science is that breadth and impartiality of view which liberates the mind from specialties, and enables it to organize whatever we learn, so that it become real Knowledge by being brought into true and helpful relation with the rest.

By far the most important change that has been introduced into the theory and practice of our teaching here by the new position in which we find ourselves has been that of the elective or voluntary system of studies. We have justified ourselves by the familiar proverb that one man may lead a horse to water, but ten can't make him drink. Proverbs are excellent things, but we should not let even proverbs bully us. They are the wisdom of the understanding, not of the higher reason. There is another animal, which even Simonides could compliment only on the spindle-side of his pedigree, and which ten men could not lead to water, much less make him drink when they got him thither. Are we not trying to force university forms into college methods too narrow for them? There is some danger that the elective system may be pushed too far and too fast. There are not a few who think that it has gone too far already. And they think so because we are in process of transformation, still in the hobbledehoy period, not having ceased to be a college, nor yet having reached the full manhood of a university, so that we speak with that ambiguous voice, half bass, half treble, or mixed of both, which is proper to a certain stage of adolescence. We are trying to do two things with one tool, and that tool not specially adapted to either. Are our students old enough thoroughly to understand the import of the choice they are called on to make, and, if old enough, are they wise enough? Shall their parents make the choice for them? I am not sure that even parents are so wise as the unbroken experience and practice of mankind. We are comforted by being told that in this we are only complying with what is called the Spirit of the Age, which may be, after all, only a finer name for the mischievous goblin known to our forefathers as Puck. I have seen several Spirits of the Age in my time, of very different voices and summoning in very different directions, but unanimous in their propensity to land us in the mire at last. Would it not be safer to make sure first whether the Spirit of the Age, who would be a very insignificant fellow if we docked him of his capitals, be not a lying spirit, since such there are? It is at least curious that, while the more advanced teaching has a strong drift in the voluntary direction, the compulsory system, as respects primary studies, is gaining ground. Is it indeed so self-

evident a proposition as it seems to many that
" You may " is as wholesome a lesson for youth as
" You must " ? Is it so good a fore-schooling for
Life, which will be a teacher of quite other mood,
making us learn, rod in hand, precisely those lessons we should not have chosen? I have, to be
sure, heard the late President Quincy (*clarum et
venerabile nomen*) say that if a young man came
hither and did nothing more than rub his shoulders
against the college buildings for four years, he
would imbibe some tincture of sound learning by
an involuntary process of absorption. The founders of the College also believed in some impul-
sions towards science communicated *â tergo* but of
sharper virtue, and accordingly armed their president with that *ductor dubitantium* which was
wielded to such good purpose by the Reverend
James Bowyer at Christ's Hospital in the days of
Coleridge and Lamb. They believed with the old
poet that whipping was " a wild benefit of nature,"
and, could they have read Wordsworth's exquisite
stanza, —

> " One impulse from a vernal wood
> Can teach us more of man,
> Of moral evil and of good,
> Than all the sages can,"

they would have struck out " vernal" and inserted
" birchen " on the margin.

I am not, of course, arguing in favor of a return
to those vapulatory methods, but the birch, like
many other things that have passed out of the region of the practical, may have another term of

usefulness as a symbol after it has ceased to be a reality.

One is sometimes tempted to think that all learning is as repulsive to ingenuous youth as the multiplication table to Scott's little friend Marjorie Fleming, though this is due in great part to mechanical methods of teaching. "I am now going to tell you," she writes, "the horrible and wretched plaege that my multiplication table gives me; you can't conceive it; the most Devilish thing is 8 times 8 and 7 times 7; it is what nature itself can't endure." I know that I am approaching treacherous ashes which cover burning coals, but I must on. Is not Greek, nay, even Latin, yet more unendurable than poor Marjorie's task? How many boys have not sympathized with Heine in hating the Romans because they invented Latin Grammar? And they were quite right, for we begin the study of languages at the wrong end, at the end which nature does not offer us, and are thoroughly tired of them before we arrive at them, if you will pardon the bull. But is that any reason for not studying them in the right way? I am familiar with the arguments for making the study of Greek especially a matter of choice or chance. I admit their plausibility and the honesty of those who urge them. I should be willing also to admit that the study of the ancient languages without the hope or the prospect of going on to what they contain would be useful only as a form of intellectual gymnastics. Even so they would be as serviceable as the higher mathematics to most of us. But I

think that a wise teacher should adapt his tasks to
the highest, and not the lowest, capacities of the
taught. For those lower also they would not be
wholly without profit. When there is a tedious
sermon, says George Herbert,

" God takes a text and teacheth patience,"

not the least pregnant of lessons. One of the arguments against the compulsory study of Greek,
namely, that it is wiser to give our time to modern
languages and modern history than to dead languages and ancient history, involves, I think, a
verbal fallacy. Only those languages can properly
be called dead in which nothing living has been
written. If the classic languages are dead, they
yet speak to us, and with a clearer voice than that
of any living tongue.

" Graiis ingenium, Graiis dedit ore rotundo
Musa loqui, præter laudem nullius avaris."

If their language is dead, yet the literature it
enshrines is rammed with life as perhaps no other
writing, except Shakespeare's, ever was or will be.
It is as contemporary with to-day as with the ears
it first enraptured, for it appeals not to the man
of then or now, but to the entire round of human
nature itself. Men are ephemeral or evanescent,
but whatever page the authentic soul of man has
touched with her immortalizing finger, no matter
how long ago, is still young and fair as it was
to the world's gray fathers. Oblivion looks in
the face of the Grecian Muse only to forget her
errand. Plato and Aristotle are not names but

things. On a chart that should represent the firm earth and wavering oceans of the human mind, they would be marked as mountain-ranges, forever modifying the temperature, the currents, and the atmosphere of thought, astronomical stations whence the movements of the lamps of heaven might best be observed and predicted. Even for the mastering of our own tongue, there is no expedient so fruitful as translation out of another ; how much more when that other is a language at once so precise and so flexible as the Greek! Greek literature is also the most fruitful comment on our own. Coleridge has told us with what profit he was made to study Shakespeare and Milton in conjunction with the Greek dramatists. It is no sentimental argument for this study that the most justly balanced, the most serene, and the most fecundating minds since the revival of learning have been steeped in and saturated with Greek literature. We know not whither other studies will lead us, especially if dissociated from this ; we do know to what summits, far above our lower region of turmoil, this has led, and what the many-sided outlook thence. Will such studies make anachronisms of us, unfit us for the duties and the business of to-day ? I can recall no writer more truly modern than Montaigne, who was almost more at home in Athens and Rome than in Paris. Yet he was a thrifty manager of his estate and a most competent mayor of Bordeaux. I remember passing once in London where demolition for a new thoroughfare was going on. Many houses left standing in the rear of those cleared away bore signs with the inscription "Ancient Lights." This was the protest of their owners against being built out by the new improvements from such glimpse of heaven as their fathers had, without adequate equivalent. I laid the moral to heart.

I am speaking of the College as it has always existed and still exists. In so far as it may be driven to put on the forms of the university, — I do not mean the four Faculties, merely, but in the modern sense, — we shall naturally find ourselves compelled to assume the method with the function. Some day we shall offer here a chance, at least, to acquire the *omne scibile.* I shall be glad, as shall we all, when the young American need no longer go abroad for any part of his training, though that may not be always a disadvantage, if Shakespeare was right in thinking that

"Home-keeping youths have ever homely wits."

I should be still gladder if Harvard should be the place that offered the alternative. It seems more than ever probable that this will happen, and happen in our day. And whenever it does happen, it will be due, more than to any and all others, to the able, energetic, single-minded, and yet fair-minded man who has presided over the College during the trying period of transition, and who will by a rare combination of eminent qualities carry that transition forward to its accomplishment without haste and without jar, — *ohne Hast, ohne Rast.* He more than any of his distinguished predecessors has brought the university into closer and more telling relations with the national life in whatever that life has which is most distinctive and most hopeful.

But we still mainly occupy the position of a German Gymnasium. Under existing circumstances, therefore, and with the methods of teaching they enforce, I think that special and advanced courses should be pushed on, so far as possible, as the other professional courses are, into the post-graduate period. The opportunity would be greater because the number would be less, and the teaching not only more thorough, but more vivifying through the more intimate relation of teacher and pupil. Under those conditions the voluntary system will not only be possible, but will come of itself, for every student will know what he wants and where he may get it, and learning will be loved, as it should be, for its own sake as well as for what it gives. The friends of university training can do nothing that would forward it more than the founding of post-graduate fellowships and the building and endowing of a hall where the holders of them might be commensals, remembering that when Cardinal Wolsey built Christ Church at Oxford his first care was the kitchen. Nothing is so great a quickener of the faculties, or so likely to prevent their being narrowed to a single groove, as the frequent social commingling of men who are aiming at one goal by different paths. If you would have really great scholars, and our life offers no prizes for such, it would be well if the university could offer them. I have often been struck with the many-sided versatility of the Fellows of English colleges who have kept their wits in training by continual fence one with another.

During the first two centuries of her existence, it may be affirmed that Harvard did sufficiently well the only work she was called on to do, perhaps the only work it was possible for her to do. She gave to Boston her scholarly impress, to the Commonwealth her scholastic impulse. To the clergy of her training was mainly intrusted the oversight of the public schools; these were, as I have said, though indirectly, feeders of the College, for their teaching was of the plainest. But if a boy in any country village showed uncommon parts, the clergyman was sure to hear of it. He and the Squire and the Doctor, if there was one, talked it over, and that boy was sure to be helped onward to college; for next to the five points of Calvinism our ancestors believed in a college education, that is, in the best education that was to be had. The system, if system it should be called, was a good one, a practical application of the doctrine of Natural Selection. Ah! how the parents — nay, the whole family — moiled and pinched that their boy might have the chance denied to them! Mr. Matthew Arnold has told us that in contemporary France, which seems doomed to try every theory of enlightenment by which the fingers may be burned or the house set on fire, the children of the public schools are taught in answer to the question, " Who gives you all these fine things ? " to say, " The State."

Ill fares the State in which the parental image is replaced by an abstraction. The answer of the boy of whom I have been speaking would have been in a spirit better for the State and for the hope of his own future life: " I owe them, under God, to my own industry, to the sacrifices of my father and mother, and to the sympathy of good men." Nor was the boy's self-respect lessened, for the aid was given by loans, to be repaid when possible. The times have changed, and it is no longer the ambition of a promising boy to go to college. They are taught to think that a common-school education is good enough for all practical purposes. And so perhaps it is, but not for all ideal purposes. Our public schools teach too little or too much: too little if education is to go no further, too many things if what is taught is to be taught thoroughly ; and the more they *seem* to teach, the less likely is education to go further, for it is one of the prime weaknesses of a democracy to be satisfied with the second-best if it appear to answer the purpose tolerably well, and to be cheaper — as it never is in the long run.

Our ancestors believed in education, but not in making it wholly eleemosynary. And they were wise in this, for men do not value what they get for nothing any more than they value air and light till deprived of them. It is quite proper that the cost of our public schools should be paid by the rich, for it is their interest, as Lord Sherbrooke said, " to educate their rulers." But it is to make paupers of the pupils to furnish them, as is now proposed, with text-books, slates, and the like at public cost. This is an advance towards that State Socialism which, if it ever prevail, will be deadly to certain homespun virtues far more precious than most of the book-knowledge in the world. It is to be hoped that our higher institutions of learning may again be brought to bear, as once they did, more directly on the lower, that they may again come into such closer and graduated relation with them as may make the higher education the goal to which all who show a clear aptitude shall aspire. I know that we cannot have ideal teachers in our public schools for the price we pay or in the numbers we require. But teaching, like water, can rise no higher than its source, and, like water again, it has a lazy aptitude for running down-hill unless a constant impulse be applied in the other direction. Would not this impulse be furnished by the ambition to send on as many pupils as possible to the wider sphere of the university? Would not this organic relation to the Higher Education necessitate a corresponding rise in the grade of intelligence, capacity, and culture demanded in the teachers?

Harvard has done much by raising its standard to force upwards that also of the preparatory schools. The leaven thus infused will, let us hope, filter gradually downwards till it raise a ferment in the lower grades as well. What we need more than anything else is to increase the number of our highly cultivated men and thoroughly trained minds; for these, wherever they go, are sure to carry with them, consciously or not, the seeds of sounder thinking and of higher ideals. The only way in which our civilization can be maintained even at the level it has reached, the only way in which that level can be made more general and be raised higher, is by bringing the influence of the more cultivated to bear with greater energy and directness on the less cultivated, and by opening more inlets to those indirect influences which make for refinement of mind and body. Democracy must show its capacity for producing not a higher average man, but the highest possible types of manhood in all its manifold varieties, or it is a failure. No matter what it does for the body, if it do not in some sort satisfy that inextinguishable passion of the soul for something that lifts life away from prose, from the common and the vulgar, it is a failure. Unless it know how to make itself gracious and winning, it is a failure. Has it done this? Is it doing this? Or trying to do it? Not yet, I think, if one may judge by that commonplace of our newspapers that an American who stays long enough in Europe is sure to find his own country unendurable when he comes back. This is not true, if I may judge from some little experience, but it is interesting as implying a certain consciousness, which is of the most hopeful augury. But we must not be impatient; it is a far cry from the dwellers in caves to even such civilization as we have achieved. I am conscious that life has been trying to civilize me for now nearly seventy years with what seem to me very inadequate results. *We* cannot afford to wait, but the Race can. And when I speak of civilization I mean those things that tend to develop the moral forces of Man, and not merely to quicken his æsthetic sensibility, though there is often a nearer relation between the two than is popularly believed.

The tendency of a prosperous Democracy — and hitherto we have had little to do but prosper — is towards an overweening confidence in itself and its home-made methods, an overestimate of material success, and a corresponding indifference to the things of the mind. The popular ideal of success seems to be more than ever before the accumulation of riches. I say "seems," for it may be only because the opportunities are greater. I am not ignorant that wealth is the great fertilizer of civilization, and of the arts that beautify it. The very names of civilization and politeness show that the refinement of manners which made the arts possible is the birth of cities, where wealth earliest accumulated because it found itself secure. Wealth may be an excellent thing, for it means power, it means leisure, it means liberty.

But these, divorced from culture, that is, from intelligent purpose, become the very mockery of their own essence, not goods, but evils fatal to their possessor, and bring with them, like the Niblung hoard, a doom instead of a blessing. A man rich only for himself has a life as barren and cheerless as that of the serpent set to guard a buried treasure. I am saddened when I see our success as a nation measured by the number of acres under tillage or bushels of wheat exported; for the real value of a country must be weighed in scales more delicate than the Balance of Trade. The garners of Sicily are empty now, but the bees from all climes still fetch honey from the tiny garden-plot of Theocritus. On a map of the world you may cover Judea with your thumb, Athens with a finger-tip, and neither of them figures in the Prices Current; but they still lord it in the thought and action of every civilized man. Did not Dante cover with his hood all that was Italy six hundred years ago? And, if we go back a century, where was Germany outside of Weimar? Material success is good, but only as the necessary preliminary of better things. The measure of a nation's true success is the amount it has contributed to the thought, the moral energy, the intellectual happiness, the spiritual hope and consolation, of mankind. There is no other, let our candidates flatter us as they may. We still make a confusion between huge and great. I know that I am repeating truisms, but they are truisms that need to be repeated in season and out of season.

The most precious property of Culture and of a college as its trustee is to maintain higher ideals of life and its purpose, to keep trimmed and burning the lamps of that pharos, built by wiser than we, which warns from the reefs and shallows of popular doctrine. In proportion as there are more thoroughly cultivated persons in a community will the finer uses of prosperity be taught and the vulgar uses of it become disreputable. And it is such

persons that we are commissioned to send out with
such consciousness of their fortunate vocation and
such devotion to it as we may. We are confronted
with unexampled problems. First of all is democracy, and that under conditions in great part novel,
with its hitherto imperfectly tabulated results,
whether we consider its effect upon national character, on popular thought, or on the functions of
law and government; we have to deal with a time
when the belief seems to be spreading that truth
not only can but should be settled by a show of
hands rather than by a count of heads, and that
one man is as good as another for all purposes, —
as, indeed, he is till a real man is needed; with a
time when the press is more potent for good or for
evil than ever any human agency was before, and
yet is controlled more than ever before, by its interests as a business rather than by its sense of
duty as a teacher, and must purvey news instead of
intelligence; with a time when divers and strange
doctrines touching the greatest human interests are
allowed to run about unmuzzled in greater number
and variety than ever before since the Reformation
passed into its stage of putrefactive fermentation;
with a time when the idols of the market-place are
more devoutly worshipped than ever Diana of the
Ephesians was; when the guilds of the Middle
Ages are revived among us with the avowed purpose of renewing by the misuse of universal suffrage the class-legislation to escape which we left
the Old World; when the electric telegraph, by
making public opinion simultaneous, is also making

it liable to those delusions, panics, and gregarious impulses which transform otherwise reasonable men into a mob; and when, above all, the better mind of the country is said to be growing more and more alienated from the highest of all sciences and services, the government of it. I have drawn up a dreary catalogue, and the moral it points is this: That the College, in so far as it continues to be still a college, as in great part it does and must, is and should be limited by certain preëxisting conditions, and must consider first what the more general objects of education are without neglecting special aptitudes more than cannot be helped. That more general purpose is, I take it, to set free, to supple, and to train the faculties in such wise as shall make them most effective for whatever task life may afterwards set them, for the duties of life rather than for its business, and to open windows on every side of the mind where thickness of wall does not prevent it.

Let our aim be, as hitherto, to give a good all-round education fitted to cope with as many exigencies of the day as possible. I had rather the College should turn out one of Aristotle's four-square men, capable of holding his own in whatever field he may be cast, than a score of lopsided ones developed abnormally in one direction. Our scheme should be adapted to the wants of the majority of under-graduates, to the objects that drew them hither, and to such training as will make the most of them after they come. Special aptitudes are sure to take care of themselves, but

the latent possibilities of the average mind can
only be discovered by experiment in many directions.   When I speak of the average mind, I do not
mean that the courses of study should be adapted
to the average level of intelligence, but to the
highest, for in these matters it is wiser to grade
upwards than downwards, since the best is the
only thing that is good enough.   To keep the
wing-footed down to the pace of the leaden-soled
disheartens the one without in the least encourag-
ing the other.   " Brains," says Machiavelli, " are
of three generations, those that understand of
themselves, those that understand when another
shows them, and those that understand neither of
themselves nor by the showing of others."   It is
the first class that should set the stint; the second
will get on better than if they had set it themselves; and the third will at least have the pleasure of watching the others show their paces.

In the College proper, I repeat, for it is the
birthday of the College that we are celebrating, it
is the College that we love and of which we are
proud, let it continue to give such a training as
will fit the rich to be trusted with riches, and the
poor to withstand the temptations of poverty.
Give to History, give to Political Economy, that
ample verge the times demand, but with no detriment to those liberal Arts which have formed open-
minded men and good citizens in the past, nor have
lost the skill to form them.   Let it be our hope to
make a gentleman of every youth who is put under
our charge ; not a conventional gentleman, but a

man of culture, a man of intellectual resource, a
man of public spirit, a man of refinement, with
that good taste which is the conscience of the mind,
and that conscience which is the good taste of the
soul. This we have tried to do in the past, this let
us try to do in the future. We cannot do this for
all, at best, — perhaps only for the few; but the
influence for good of a highly trained intelligence
and a harmoniously developed character is incalculable; for though it be subtle and gradual in its
operation, it is as pervasive as it is subtle. There
may be few of these, there must be few, but

> " That few is all the world which with a few
>   Doth ever live and move and work and stirre."

If these few can best be winnowed from the rest
by the elective system of studies, if the drift of our
colleges towards that system be general and involuntary, showing a demand for it in the conditions
of American life, then I should wish to see it un-
falteringly carried through. I am sure that the
matter will be handled wisely and with all forethought by those most intimately concerned in the
government of the College.

They who, on a tiny clearing pared from the
edge of the woods, built here, most probably with
the timber hewed from the trees they felled, our
earliest hall, with the solitude of ocean behind
them, the mystery of forest before them, and all
about them a desolation, must surely (*si quis ani-
mis celestibis locus*) share our gladness and our
gratitude at the splendid fulfilment of their vision.
If we could but have preserved the humble roof

which housed so great a future, Mr. Ruskin himself would almost have admitted that no castle or
cathedral was ever richer in sacred associations,
in pathos of the past, and in moral significance.
They who reared it had the sublime prescience of
that courage which fears only God, and could say
confidently in the face of all discouragement and
doubt, " He hath led me forth into a large place ;
because he delighted in me, He hath delivered me."
We cannot honor them too much ; we can repay
them only by showing, as occasions rise, that we do
not undervalue the worth of their example.

Brethren of the Alumni, it now becomes my
duty to welcome in your name the guests who have
come, some of them so far, to share our congratulations and hopes to-day. I cannot name them all
and give to each his fitting phrase. Thrice welcome to them all, and, as is fitting, first to those
from abroad, representatives of illustrious seats of
learning that were old in usefulness and fame when
ours was in its cradle ; and next to those of our
own land, from colleges and universities which, if
not daughters of Harvard, are young enough to be
so, and are one with her in heart and hope. I said
that I should single out none by name, but I should
not represent you fitly if I gave no special greeting
to the gentleman who brings the message of John
Harvard's College, Emmanuel. The welcome we
give him could not be warmer than that which
we offer to his colleagues, but we cannot help feeling that in pressing his hand our own instinctively
closes a little more tightly, as with a sense of nearer

kindred. There is also one other name of which
it would be indecorous not to make an exception.
You all know that I can mean only the President
of our Republic. His presence is a signal honor
to us all, and to us all I may say a personal grati-
fication. We have no politics here, but the sons of
Harvard all belong to the party which admires
courage, strength of purpose, and fidelity to duty,
and which respects, wherever he may be found, the

> " Justum ac tenacem propositi virum,"

who knows how to withstand the

> " Civium ardor prava jubentium."

He has left the helm of state to be with us here,
and so long as it is intrusted to his hands we are
sure that, should the storm come, he will say with
Seneca's Pilot, "O Neptune, you may save me if
you will ; you may sink me if you will ; but whatever happen, I shall keep my rudder true."

TARIFF REFORM

ADDRESS AT A MEETING OF THE TARIFF REFORM
LEAGUE, BOSTON, DECEMBER 29, 1887.

GENTLEMEN: In what I have to say (and it will
not tax your patience long) I shall discreetly confine myself to generalities. These are apt, I know,
to flatten into platitudes, unless handled with practical dexterity. But I had rather run the risk of
this than abuse the chairman's privilege of speaking first, as I have sometimes seen it abused to my
own detriment. I shall be careful not to devas-
tate the speeches of those who are to come after
me by trying to show how many fine things I can
say about the subject which will be the chief topic
of discussion to-night. I shall prefer to let you
suppose that I could say them if I would. For I
consider the true office of a chairman on such
occasions to be that of the heralds who blow a few
conventional notes to announce that the lists are
open.

At this season, which custom has set apart for
mutual good wishes and felicitations, members of a
common kindred are wont to accentuate the feeling
that is in all hearts by gathering round a board
whose good cheer is at once the symbol and the
stimulant of the generous sympathies within. Our

festival seems to be prettily analogous with those others more peculiar to the season. For there are affinities of sentiment, there is a kinship of thought, and of the opinions and conduct that come of think-ing, which often bind men together more closely than ties of blood. We are, it is true, of kin to each other as the children of a common country, but we are more nearly related, we are more vitally stirred by a consent of judgment in what we be-lieve to be for the honor and the welfare of the Mother so dear to us all.

This is no doubt a political meeting; but most of you would not be here, I certainly should not be here, had this been a conspiracy in the interest of any party or of any faction within a party, had it been, that is to say, political in that ill sense which our practice, if not our theory, has given to what should be the noblest exercise of man's intellect and the best training of his character. I believe, and am glad to believe, that all shades of party allegiance are represented here. If, in a free com-monwealth, government by party be a necessary expedient, it also is a necessary evil, an evil chiefly in this, that it enables men, nay, even forces them, to postpone interests of prime import and conse-quence to secondary and ephemeral, often to per-sonal interests, and not only so, but to confound one with the other. The success of the party be-comes only too soon of more importance than that of any principles it may be supposed to have or to profess. Is not the main use of a party platform that a screen may be built of its planks to hide its principles from every profane eye? Has not the youngest of us seen parties repeatedly "change sides" with the airy gravity of a country dance? Our party arrangements and contrivances are grown so intricate, too frequently so base, that the management of them has become a gainful profession, and the class of men who should shape public opinion and control the practical application of it, are reduced to handing the highest duty the State has entrusted them with to attorneys, not of their own choice, whose hands are not too delicate to be dipped into the nauseous mess with which they are too fastidious to soil their own. I do not believe that there is a man at this table who for the last twenty years has been able to embody his honest opinion, or even a fraction of it, in his vote. During all those years no thoughtful man has been able to see any other difference between the two great parties which stood between him and the reforms he deemed essential to the well being of his country than that the one was *in* and wished to stay there, and the other was *out* and *did n't* wish to stay there. Each appeared to make use of the same unworthy tricks for its own immediate advantage, each had an abundance of aces in its sleeve, and each was divided on the two great questions of vital interest to the country, the tariff and finance. If our politicians would devote to the study and teaching of political economy half the time they spend in trying to agree so as not to agree with the latest attempt of the Knights of Labor to unhorse the Nature of Things, they would be far less harm-

ful to themselves and to the country.   Party allegiance tends naturally to concentrate upon some
representative or available man, and from this to
degenerate into a policy of the strongest lungs, by
which voters are driven, as sheep are driven,
blinded by the dust themselves have raised, to over-
trample whatever obstacle of prudence or reflection
may stand in their way.   Have we not more than
once seen men nominated for the highest office of
the State because they had no " record," as it is
called, that is, men with no opinion that could be
found out, but who would serve as well as another
(under strict supervision) to divide the booty?
Nothing will ever persuade me that the American
people would select such men as the representatives of their ideal, if they could help it.   It is the
duty of all sedate and thoughtful people to help
them to help it by every honest means; if party be
a miserable necessity, it is the business of all such
to mitigate, if they cannot nullify, its evils whenever they have the chance.

One, certainly, of the reasons which have brought
us hither, one, at least, of those that chiefly suggested the opportuneness of our coming together
here, has been the President's message at the opening of the present Congress.   Personally, I confess
that I feel myself strongly attracted to Mr. Cleveland as the best representative of the higher type
of Americanism that we have seen since Lincoln
was snatched from us.   And by Americanism I
mean that which we cannot help, not that which
we flaunt, that way of looking at things and of

treating men which we derive from the soil that holds our fathers and waits for us. I think we have all recognized in him a manly simplicity of character and an honest endeavor to do all that he could of duty, when all that he would was made impossible by difficulties to the hourly trials and temptations of which we have fortunately never been exposed. But we are not here to thank him as the head of a party. We are here to felicitate each other that the presidential chair has a MAN in it, and this means that every word he *says* is weighted with what he *is*. We are here to felicitate each other that this man understands politics to mean business, not chicanery; plain speaking, not paltering with us in a double sense ; that he has had the courage to tell the truth to the country without regard to personal or party consequences, and thus to remind us that a country not worth telling the truth to is not worth living in, nay, deserves to have lies told it, and to take the inevitable consequences in calamity. If it be lamentable that acts of official courage should have become so rare among us as to be noteworthy, it is consoling to believe that they are sometimes contagious. " So shines a good deed in a naughty world ! " As courage is preëminently the virtue of men, so it is the virtue which most powerfully challenges the respect and emulation of men. And it deserves this preëminence, for it is also the virtue which gives security to all the other virtues. We thank the President for having taught a most pertinent object lesson, and from a platform lofty enough to be seen of all the people. We should be glad to think, though we hardly dare to hope, that some of the waiters on popular providence whom we humorously call statesmen would profit by it. As one of the evil phenomena which are said to mark the advances of democracy is the decay of civic courage, we should be grateful to the President for giving us reason to think that this is rather one of its accidents than of its properties. Whatever be the effect of Mr. Cleveland's action on his personal fortunes, let us rejoice to think it will be a stimulating thorn in that august chair for all that may sit in it after him. Would that all our presidents might see and lay to heart that vision which Dion saw, that silent shape of woman sweeping and ever sweeping without pause. Our politics call loudly for a broom. There are rubbish-heaps of cant in every corner of them that should be swept out for the dustman Time to cart away and dump beyond sight or smell of mortal man. Mr. Cleveland, I think, has found the broom and begun to ply it.

But, gentlemen, the President has set us an example not only of courage, but of good sense and moderation. He has kept strictly to his text and his purpose. He has stated the facts and marshalled the figures without drawing further inferences from them than were implicitly there. He has confined himself to the economic question, to that which directly concerns the national housekeeping. He has not allowed himself to be lured from the direct forthright by any temptation to discuss the more general and at present mainly academic questions of free trade or protection. He has shown us that there was such a thing as being protected too much, and that we had protected our shipping interests so effectually that they had ceased to need protection by ceasing to exist. In thus limiting the field of his warning and his counsels he has done wisely, and we shall do wisely in following his example. His facts and his figures will work all the more effectually. But we must be patient with them and expect them to work slowly. Enormous interests are involved and must be treated tenderly. It was sixty years before the leaven of Adam Smith impregnated the whole sluggish lump of British opinion, and we are a batch of the same dough. I can remember the time when bounties were paid for the raising of wheat in Massachusetts. Bounties have fallen into discredit now. They have taken an alias and play their three-card trick as subsidies or as protection to labor, but the common sense of our people will find them out at last. If we are not to expect any other immediate result from the message than that best result of all human speech, that it awaken thought, one can at least already thank it for one signal and unquestionable benefit. It is dividing, and will continue more and more to divide, our parties by the lines of natural cleavage, and will close the artificial and often mischievous lines which followed the boundaries of section or the tracings of bygone prejudices. We have here a question which equally concerns every man, woman, and child, black or white, from the Atlantic to the Pacific, from the Gulf of Mexico to the Bay of Fundy. We have here a topic which renders nugatory all those problems of ancient history which we debated and settled more than twenty years ago by manly wager of battle, and that so definitely that we welcome here to-night with special pleasure some of the brave men with whom we argued them, and whom we insisted all the more on keeping as countrymen, that they had taught us how to value them.

Gentlemen, I think I have occupied as much of your time as a chairman should. I will only ask your patience while I detain you for a moment longer from other speakers, whom I am as eager to hear as you must be. The allusion to our civil war, which I made a moment ago, suggests to me a thought which I should be glad to share with you before I close. That tremendous convulsion, as, I believe, even those engaged on the losing side now see as clearly as we, saved us a country that was worth saving, so that properly there *was* no losing side. Now what I wish to say is this, that a country worth saving is worth saving all the time, and that a country with such energies as ours, with such opportunities and inducements to grow rich, and such temptations to be content with growing rich, *needs* saving all the time. Many of us remember, as they remember nothing else, the overwhelming rush of that great national passion, obliterating all lines of party division and levelling all the landmarks of habitual politics. Who that saw it will ever forget that enthusiasm of loyalty for the flag and for what the flag symbolized which

twenty-six years ago swept all the country's forces
of thought and sentiment, of memory and hope, into
the grasp of its overmastering torrent?   Martial
patriotism touches the heart, kindles the imagination, and rouses the nobler energies of men as nothing else ever does or can.   Even love is a paler
emotion.   That image of our Country with the
flame of battle in her eyes which every man then
saw, how beautiful it was, how potent to inspire
devotion!   But these ecstasies of emotion are by
their very nature as transient as they are ennobling.
There is a sedater kind of patriotism, less picturesque, less inspiring, but quite as admirably serviceable in the prosy days of peace.   It is the
patient patriotism which strives to enlighten public
opinion and to redress the balance of party spirit,
which inculcates civic courage and independence of
mind, which refuses to accept clamor as argument,
or to believe that phrases become syllogisms by
repetition.   It is this more modest and thoughtful patriotism to the exemplifying and practice of
which we aspire, and the first lesson it teaches us
is that a moderated and controlled enthusiasm is,
like stored electricity, the most powerful of motive
forces, and that the reformer of practical abuses,
springing from economic ignorance or mistake, then
first begins to be wise when he allows for the
obstinate vitality of human error and human folly,
and is willing to believe that those who cannot see
as he does are not therefore necessarily bad men.

THE PLACE OF THE INDEPENDENT IN POLITICS.

AN ADDRESS DELIVERED BEFORE THE REFORM CLUB OF
NEW YORK, AT STEINWAY HALL, APRIL 13, 1888.

I HAVE not been so much surprised as perhaps I
ought to have been to learn that, in the opinion of
some of our leading politicians and of many of
our newspapers, men of scholarly minds are *ipso
facto* debarred from forming any judgment on public affairs; or, if they should be so unscrupulous
as to do so, that they must at least refrain from
communicating it to their fellow-citizens. One
eminent gentleman has even gone so far as to sneer
at school-books as sources of information. If he
had a chance, he would perhaps take a hint from
what is fabled of the Caliph Omar, and burn our
libraries: because if they contained doctrine not to
be found in his speeches, they would be harmful,
while if the doctrine, judged by that test, were
orthodox, they would be useless. Books have
hitherto been supposed to be armories of human
experience, where we might equip ourselves for
the battles of opinion while we had yet vigor and
hopefulness enough left to make our weapons of
some avail.

Through books the youngest of us could converse with more generations than Nestor; could attain that ripened judgment which is the privilege of old age without old age's drawbacks and dimi-nutions. This has been the opinion of many men, not reckoned the least wise in their generation. But they were mistaken, it seems. I looked round with saddened wonder at the costly apparatus of school-houses provided by our ancestors to the avowed end that "good learning might not cease from among us," at the libraries and universities by the founding of which our rich men seek to atone for their too rapidly agglomerated wealth, and said to myself, "What a wasteful blunder we have been making!" Then it suddenly occurred to me that this putting of culture under the ban might be, after all, but a more subtle application of the American system, as it is called, which would exclude all foreign experience, as well as the raw material of it, till we had built up an ex-perience of our own at the same cost of mistake and retribution which is its unvarying price. This might indeed flatter my pride of country, though it left me, as Grumio says, to "return unexperienced to my grave."

But if we are forbidden to seek knowledge in books, what is the alternative? I could think of none unless it were immediate inspiration. It is true that I could not see that any authentic marks of it were revealed by the advocates of this novel theory. They keep their secret remarkably well. No doubt inspiration, like money, is a very handy thing to have, and if I should ever see an advertisement of any shop where it could be bought, even at second hand, I would lay in a stock of it forthwith. It is more convenient than knowledge, for, like certain articles of wearing apparel, it is adjustable to the prevailing taste of the moment in any part of the country. It seems more studious of the traditions and prejudices of the multitude than the utterances of Isaiah were wont to be. I must frankly confess at the outset that I come to you wholly unprovided with this precious commodity. I must also admit that I am a book-man, that I am old-fashioned enough to have read many books, and that I hope to read many more. I find them easier reading than some other kinds of printed matter. I appear before you, therefore, with some diffidence, and shall make my excuses in the words of an elder who in my youth was accounted wise. Lord Bacon, a man versed both in affairs and in books, says: " And for the matter of policy and government, that learning should rather hurt than enable thereunto is a thing very improbable. We see it is accounted an error to commit a natural body to empiric physicians who commonly have a few pleasing receipts whereupon they are confident and adventurous, but know neither the causes of diseases, nor the constitutions of patients, nor peril of accidents, nor the true method of cures ; we see it is a like error to rely upon advocates or lawyers who are only men of practice and not grounded in their books, who are many times easily surprised when matter falleth out beyond their experience to the prejudice of the causes they handle ; so by like

reason it cannot be but a matter of doubtful consequence if states be managed by empiric statesmen not well mingled with men grounded in learning. But, contrariwise, it is almost without an
instance to the contrary that ever any government
was disastrous that was in the hands of learned
governors." He goes on to say that " It hath been
ordinary with politique men to extenuate and dis-
able learned men by the name of *pedants*." Practical politicians, as they call themselves, have the
same habit still, only that they have substituted
doctrinaire for *pedant* as the term of reproach.
Now the true and mischievous doctrinaire is he
who insists that facts shall accommodate themselves
to preconceived theory, and the truly practical man
he who would deduce theory from the amplest possible comparison and correlation of facts; in other
words, from recorded experience. I think it is
already beginning to be apparent on which side of
the questions which have been brought to the front
by the President's Message the doctrinaires are to
be found. We all know the empiric physicians
who are confident and adventurous with their few
pleasing receipts.

Your committee asked me to give a title to such
suggestions as I might find occasion to make this
evening, and I took " The Place of the Independent in Politics " as the first that occurred to me.
But I confess that I partake of Mr. Walter Shan-
dy's superstition about names, and shall not allow
myself to be circumscribed and scanted of elbow-
room by the appellative I have chosen. I prefer

general to personal politics. I allude to this in order that, in anything I shall say here, I may not be suspected to have one party more than another in my mind. I am not blind to the fact that Truth always seems to have gone to school to the prophet Nathan, and to intend a personal application. It is perhaps her prime virtue as a stimulant of thought, for thought is helpful in proportion as it more and more becomes disengaged from self, and this cannot happen till some sharp reminder makes us conscious of that plausible accomplice in our thinking and in the doing which follows from it. Though I shall not evade present questions when they come naturally in my way, I shall choose rather to indicate why there is a necessity that the Independent should have a place in politics than to dictate where that place should be. I think that something I wrote forty years ago, if you will allow me to quote it, will define my notion of what is meant by an Independent with sufficient exactness. I then said, and I have not changed my mind : —

> I honor the man who is ready to sink
> Half his present repute for the freedom to think,
> And when he has thought, be his cause strong or weak,
> Will risk 't other half for the freedom to speak,
> Caring naught for what vengeance the mob has in store,
> Let that mob be the upper ten thousand or lower.

Four years ago I was called upon to deliver an address in Birmingham, and chose for my theme "Democracy." In that place I felt it incumbent on me to dwell on the good points and favorable aspects of democracy as I had seen them practically illustrated in my native land. I chose rather

that my discourse should suffer through inadequacy
than run the risk of seeming to forget what Burke
calls "that salutary prejudice called our country,"
and that obligation which forbids one to discuss
family affairs before strangers. But here among
ourselves it is clearly the duty of whoever loves
his country to be watchful of whatever weaknesses
and perils there may be in the practical working
of a system never before set in motion under such
favorable auspices, or on so large a scale. I have
called them· weaknesses and perils in the system,
but it would be idle to discuss them if I did not
believe that they were not so properly results of
the system as of abuses in the operation of it, due
in part to changed conditions, in part to a thought-
less negligence which experience and thought will
in due time rectify. I believe that no other method
of conducting the public affairs of men is so capable of sloughing off its peccant parts as ours, because in no other are the forces of life at once so
intense and so universally distributed.

Before we turn to the consideration of politics
as we see them in practice, let us think for a moment what, when properly understood, they really
are. In their least comprehensive definition, politics
are an art which concerns itself about the national
housekeeping, about the immediate interests and
workaday wants, the income and the outgo of the
people. They have to deal with practical questions as they arise and grow pressing. Even on
this humbler plane they may well have an attrac-
tion for the finest intellects and the greatest abili-

ties in a country where public opinion is supreme, for they can perform their function only by persuading, convincing, and thus governing the minds of men. The most trivial question acquires dignity when it touches the well-being or rouses the passions of many millions. But there is a higher and wider sense in which politics may fairly be ranked as a science. When they rise to this level we call them statesmanship. The statesman applies himself to the observation and recording of certain causes which lead constantly to certain effects, and is thus able to formulate general laws for the guidance of his own judgment and for the conduct of affairs. He is not so much interested in the devices by which men *may* be influenced, as about how they *ought* to be influenced; not so much about how men's passions and prejudices may be utilized for a momentary advantage to himself or his party, as about how they may be hindered from doing a permanent harm to the commonwealth. He trains himself to discern evils in their causes that he may forewarn if he cannot prevent, and that he may not be taken unawares by the long bill of damages they are sure to bring in, and always at the least convenient moment. He seeks and finds in the moral world the weather-signs of the actual world. He strives to see and know things as they really are and as they are related to each other, as they really are and therefore always must be; his vision undeflected by the cross-lights of transitory circumstance, his judgment undisturbed by the clamor of passionate and changeful opinion.

That this conception of statesmanship is not fanciful, the writings and speeches of Burke are ample proof. Many great and many acute minds had speculated upon politics from Aristotle's time downwards, but Burke was the first to illuminate the subject of his observation and thought with the electric light of imagination. He turned its penetrating ray upon what seemed the confused and wavering cloud-chaos of man's nature and man's experience, and found there the indication, at least, if not the scheme, of a divine order. The result is that his works are as full of prophecy, some of it already fulfilled, some of it in course of fulfilment, as they are of wisdom. And this is because for him human nature was always the text and history the comment. There are no more pregnant lessons in the science of how to look at things so as to see them and into them, of how to distinguish what is perennial from what is deciduous in a political question, than Burke's two speeches on " Taxation of the American Colonies" and on "Conciliation with America." For if his imagination was fervid, it served but to warm his understanding till that grew ductile enough to take a perfect impression of fact. If the one made generalization easy, the other, in testing the generalization, compelled him always to make account of the special diagnosis of the case in hand. If one would know the difference between a statesman and a politician, let him compare Burke's view of the American troubles with that of Dr. Johnson, a man of that headstrong common sense which sees with absorbing, one might

almost say blinding, clearness whatever comes
within its immediate field of vision, but is conscious of nothing beyond it.   The question for
Burke was not whether taxation were tyranny,
but whether the Americans would think it so.
Here was a case in which expediency was at one
with wisdom.

But I am happy in being able to find an illustration nearer home.   Never did three men show
more clearly the quality of true statesmanship or
render a more precious service to their country
than Senators Fessenden, Trumbull, and Grimes,
when they dared to act independently of party in
the impeachment case against President Johnson.
They saved us from the creeping paralysis which
is now gradually benumbing the political energies
of France.   Nay, while we were yet in the gristle,
we produced statesmen, not, indeed, endowed with
Burke's genius, though fairly comparable with him
in breadth of view, and sometimes his superiors
in practical sagacity.   But I think there is a growing doubt whether we are not ceasing to produce
them, whether perhaps we are not losing the power
to produce them.   The tricks of management are
more and more superseding the science of government.   Our methods force the growth of two kinds
of politicians to the crowding out of all other varieties, — him who is called *practical*, and him of the
corner grocery.   The one trades in that counterfeit
of public opinion which the other manufactures.
Both work in the dark, and there is need that
some one should turn the light of his policeman's

lantern on their doings. I believe that there is as much of the raw material of statesmanship among us as ever there was, but the duties levied by the local rings of majority-manufacturers are so high as to prohibit its entrance into competition with the protected article. Could we only have a travelling exhibition of our Bosses, and say to the American people, " Behold the shapers of your national destiny ! " A single despot would be cheaper, and probably better looking. It is a natural impulse to turn away one's eyes from these flesh-flies that fatten on the sores of our body politic, and plant there the eggs of their disgustful and infectious progeny. But it is the lesson of the day that a yielding to this repulsion by the intelligent and refined is a mainly efficient cause of the evil, and must be overcome, at whatever cost of selfish ease and æsthetic comfort, ere the evil can be hopefully dealt with.

It is admitted on all hands that matters have been growing worse for the last twenty years, as it is the nature of evil to do. It is publicly asserted that admission to the Senate of the United States is a marketable thing. I know not whether this be true or not, but is it not an ominous sign of the times that this has been asserted and generally believed to be possible, if not probable ? It is notorious that important elections are decided by votes bought with money, or by the more mischievous equivalent of money, places in the public service. What is even more disheartening, the tone of a large part of the press in regard to this state of things is cynical, or even jocular. And how often do we not read in our morning paper that such and such a local politician is dictating the choice of delegates to a nominating convention, or manipulating them after they are chosen? So often that we at last take it as a matter of course, as something beyond our power to modify or control, like the weather, at which we may grumble, if we like, but cannot help. We should not tolerate a packed jury which is to decide on the fate of a single man, yet we are content to leave the life of the nation at the mercy of a packed convention. We allow ourselves to be bilked of our rights and thwarted in our duties as citizens by men in whose hands their very henchmen would be the last to trust anything more valuable than their reputation. Pessimists tell us that these things are the natural incidents and necessary consequences of representative government under democratic conditions; that we have drawn the wine, and must drink it. If I believed this to be so, I should not be speaking here to-night. Parties refuse to see, or, if they see, to look into, vicious methods which help them to a majority, and each is thus estopped from sincere protest against the same methods when employed by the other. The people of the Northern States thought four years' war not too dear a price to prevent half their country being taken from them. But the practices of which I have been speaking are slowly and surely filching from us the whole of our country, — all, at least, that made it the best to live in and the easiest to die for. If

parties will not look after their own drainage and
ventilation, there must be people who will do it for
them, who will cry out without ceasing till their fellow-citizens are aroused to the danger of infection.
This duty can be done only by men dissociated
from the interests of party. The Independents
have undertaken it, and with God's help will carry
it through. A moral purpose multiplies us by ten,
as it multiplied the early Abolitionists. They
emancipated the negro; and we mean to emancipate the respectable white man.

It is time for lovers of their country to consider
how much of the success of our experiment in democracy has been due to such favorable conditions
as never before concurred to make such an attempt
plausible; whether those conditions have changed
and are still changing for the worse; how far we
have been accessories in this degeneration, if such
there be, and how far it is in our power, with the
means furnished by the very instruments of destruction, to stay its advance and to repair its rav-
ages. Till within a few years of our civil war,
everything conduced to our measuring the success of our institutions by the evidence of our outward prosperity, and to our seeing the future in
rose-color. The hues of our dawn had scarcely
faded from the sky. Men were still living who
had seen the face and heard the voice of the most
august personage in our history, and of others
scarce less august than he. The traditions of our
founders were fresh. Our growth in wealth and
power was without precedent. We had been so

fortunate that we had come to look upon our luck as partly due to our own merits and partly to our form of government. When we met together it was to felicitate each other on our superiority to the rest of mankind. Our ears caught from behind the horizon the muffled thunders of war, only to be lulled as with the murmurs of the surf on a far-off shore. We heard of revolutions, but for us Fortune forgot to turn her wheel. This was what may be called the Fourth of July period of our history. Among the peoples of the earth we were the little Jack Horner. We had put in our thumb and pulled out a plum, and the rest of mankind thought that we were never tired of saying, " What a good boy am I ! " Here is a picture of our growth, drawn by a friendly yet impartial hand : " Nothing in the history of mankind is like their progress. For my part, I never cast an eye on their flourishing commerce and their cultivated and commodious life but they seem to me rather ancient nations grown to perfection through a long series of fortunate events and a train of successful industry accumulating wealth in many centuries than the colonies of yesterday. . . . Your children do not grow faster from infancy to manhood than they spread from families to communities, and from villages to nations." But for a certain splendor of style these words seem to be of yesterday, so pertinent are they still. They were uttered in the British Parliament more than a year before the battle of Lexington, by Edmund Burke. There is no exaggeration in them. They are a simple statement of fact.

Burke, with his usual perspicacity, saw and stated one and a chief cause of this unprecedented phenomenon. He tells us that the colonies had made this marvellous growth because, "through a wise and salutary neglect, a generous nature has been suffered to take her own way to perfection." But by that " wise and salutary, neglect " he meant freedom from the petty and short-sighted meddlesomeness of a paternal government; he meant being left to follow untrammelled the instincts of our genius under the guidance of our energy. The same causes have gone on ever since working the same marvels. Those marvels have been due in part to our political system. But there were other circumstances tending to stimulate personal energy and enterprise, especially land to be had for the taking, and free trade over a larger share of the earth's surface peopled by thriving and intelligent communities than had ever been enjoyed elsewhere. I think, however, that there was one factor more potent than any other, or than all others together. Before we broke away from the mother country politically, a century and a half of that " wise neglect " of which Burke spoke had thoroughly made over again and Americanized all the descendants of the earlier settlers, and these formed the great bulk of the population. The same process was rapidly going on in the more recent immigrants. So thorough had this process been that many, perhaps most, of the refugees who, during or after the Revolutionary War, went to England, or home, as they fondly called it, found themselves out of place and unhappy there. The home they missed was that humane equality, not of condition or station, but of being and opportunity, which by some benign influence of the place had overcome them here, like a summer cloud, without their special wonder. Yet they felt the comfort of it as of an air wholesome to breathe. I more than suspect that it was the absence of this inestimable property of the moral atmosphere that made them aliens in every other land, and convinced them that an American can no more find another country than a second mother. This equality had not then been proclaimed as a right; it had been incorporated in no constitution, but was there by the necessity of the case — a gift of the sky and of the forest, as truly there as it now is in that great West whose history was so admirably treated by Senator Hoar a few days ago, and whose singular good-fortune it has been that no disparities except those of nature's making have ever been known there. Except in the cities of the seaboard, where the habits of the Old World had to some extent been kept alive by intercourse and importation, the defecation of the body politic and the body social of all purely artificial and arbitrary distinctions had been going on silently and surely among the masses of the people for generations. This was true (in a more limited sense) even of communities where slavery existed, for as that was based on complexion, every white, no matter what his condition, belonged to the privileged class, just as in Hungary every Magyar was a noble. This was the American novelty, no bant-

ling of theory, no fruit of forethought, no trophy
of insurgent violence, but a pure evolution from
the nature of man in a perfectly free medium.
The essential triumph was achieved in this tacit
recognition of a certain privilege and adequacy
in mere manhood, and democracy may be said to
have succeeded before it was accepted as doctrine
or embodied as a political fact. Our ancestors
sought a new country. What they found was a
new condition of mind. It is more than questionable whether the same conditions in as favorable
combination of time and place will ever occur
again, whether equality, so wholesome when a social evolution, as I have described it, may not
become harmful as a sudden gift in the form of
dogma, may not indeed prove dangerous when interpreted and applied politically by millions of
newcomers alien to our traditions, unsteadied by
lifelong training and qualifying associations. We
have great and thus far well-warranted faith in the
digestive and assimilative powers of our system;
but may not these be overtaxed?

The theory of equality was as old, among men
of English blood, as Jack Cade's rebellion, but it
was not practically conceived even by the very men
who asserted it. Here, on the edge of the forest,
where civilized man was brought face to face again
with nature and taught to rely mainly on himself,
mere manhood became a fact of prime importance.
That century and a half of apprenticeship in democracy stimulated self-help, while it also necessi-
tated helpfulness for others and mutual dependence

upon them. Not without reason did "help" take the place of "servant" in our vocabulary. But the conditions of life led to other results that left less salutary effects behind them. They bred a habit of contentment with what would *do*, as we say, rather than an impatience of whatever was not best; a readiness to put up with many evils or inconveniences, because they could not be helped; and this has, especially in our politics, conduced to the growth of the greatest weakness in our American character — the acquiescence in makeshifts and abuses which can and ought to be helped, and which, with honest resolution, might be helped.

Certainly never were the auguries so favorable as when our republic was founded, a republic sure from inherent causes to broaden into a more popular form. But while the equality of which I have been speaking existed in the instincts, the habits, and obscurely in the consciousness of all, it was latent and inert. It found little occasion for self-assertion, none for aggression, and was slow to invent one. A century ago there was still a great respect for authority in all its manifestations; for the law first of all, for age, for learning, and for experience. The community recognized and followed its natural leaders, and it was these who framed our Constitution, perhaps the most remarkable monument of political wisdom known to history. The convention which framed it was composed of the choicest material in the community, and was led astray by no theories of what *might* be good, but clave closely to what experience had demonstrated to *be* good.

The late M. Guizot once asked me "how long I thought our republic would endure." I replied: "So long as the ideas of the men who founded it continue dominant," and he assented. I will not say that we could not find among us now the constituents of as able an assembly, but I doubt if there be a single person in this audience who believes that with our present political methods we should or could elect them. We have revived the English system of rotten boroughs, under which the electors indeed return the candidate, but it is a handful of men, too often one man, that selects the person to be so returned. If this be so, and I think it is so, it should give us matter for very serious reflection.

After our Constitution got fairly into working order it really seemed as if we had invented a machine that would go of itself, and this begot a faith in our luck which even the civil war itself but momentarily disturbed. Circumstances continued favorable, and our prosperity went on increasing. I admire the splendid complacency of my countrymen, and find something exhilarating and inspiring in it. We are a nation which has *struck ile*, but we are also a nation that is sure the well will never run dry. And this confidence in our luck with the absorption in material interests, generated by unparalleled opportunity, has in some respects made us neglectful of our political duties. I have long thought that the average men of our revolutionary period were better grounded in the elementary principles of government than their de-

scendants.   The town-meeting was then a better
training-school than the caucus and the convention
are now, and the smaller the community the greater
the influence of the better mind in it.   In looking
about me, I am struck with the fact that while we
produce great captains, financial and industrial
leaders in abundance, and political managers in
overabundance, there seems to be a pause in the
production of leaders in statesmanship.   I am still
more struck with the fact that my newspaper often
gives me fuller reports of the speeches of Prince
Bismarck and of Mr. Gladstone than of anything
said in Congress.   If M. Thiers or M. Gambetta
were still here, it would be the same with them;
but France, like ourselves, has gone into the manufacture of small politicians.   Why are we interested
in what these men say?   Because they are important for what they *are*, as well as for what they
represent.   They are Somebodies, and their every
word gathers force from the character and life
behind it.   They stand for an idea as well as for
a constituency.   An adequate amount of small
change will give us the equivalent of the largest
piece of money, but what aggregate of little men
will amount to a single great one, that most precious coinage of the mint of nature?   It is not that
we have lost the power of bringing forth great
men.   They are not the ·product of institutions,
though these may help or hinder them.   I am
thankful to have been the contemporary of one and
among the greatest, of whom I think it is safe
to say that no other country and no other form of

government could have fashioned him, and whom posterity will recognize as the wisest and most bravely human of modern times. It is a benediction to have lived in the same age and in the same country with Abraham Lincoln.

Had democracy borne only this consummate flower and then perished like the century-plant, it would have discharged its noblest function. It is the crown of a nation, one might almost say the chief duty of a nation, to produce great men, for without them its history is but the annals of ants and bees. Two conditions are essential : the man, and the opportunity. We must wait on Mother Nature for the one, but in America we ourselves can do much to make or mar the other. We cannot always afford to set our house on fire as we did for Lincoln, but we are certainly responsible if the door to distinction be made so narrow and so low as to admit only petty and crouching men.

A democracy makes certain duties incumbent on every citizen which under other forms of government are limited to a man or to a class of men. A prudent despot looks after his kingdom as a prudent private man would look after his estate ; in an aristocratic republic a delegated body of nobles manages public affairs as a board of railroad directors would manage the property committed to their charge ; in both cases, self-interest is strong enough to call forth every latent energy of character and intellect; in both cases the individual is so consciously important a factor as to insure a sense of personal responsibility. In the ancient democracies a citizen could see and feel the effect of his own vote. But in a democracy so vast as ours, though the responsibility be as great (I remember an election in which the governor of a State was chosen by a majority of one vote), yet the infinitesimal division of power wellnigh nullifies the sense of it, and of the responsibility implied in it. It is certainly a great privilege to have a direct share in the government of one's country, but it is a privilege which is of advantage to the commonwealth only in proportion as it is intelligently exercised. Then, indeed, its constant exercise should train the faculties of forethought and judgment better, and should give men a keener sense of their own value than perhaps anything else can do. But under every form of representative government, parties become necessary for the marshalling and expression of opinion, and, when parties are once formed, those questions the discussion of which would discipline and fortify men's minds tend more and more to pass out of sight, and the topics that interest their prejudices and passions to become more absorbing. What will be of immediate advantage to the party is the first thing considered, what of permanent advantage to their country the last. I refer especially to neither of the great parties which divide the country. I am treating a question of natural history. Both parties have been equally guilty, both have evaded, as successfully as they could, the living questions of the day. As the parties have become more evenly balanced, the difficulty of arriving at their opinions has been greater in pro-

portion to the difficulty of devising any profession
of faith meaningless enough not to alarm, if it
could not be so interpreted as to conciliate, the
varied and sometimes conflicting interests of the
different sections of the country. If you asked
them, as *Captain Standard* in Farquahar's comedy
asks *Parley*, "Have you any principles?" the answer, like his, would have been, "Five hundred."
Between the two a conscientious voter feels as the
traveller of fifty years ago felt between the touters
of the two rival hotels in the village where the
stage-coach stopped for dinner. Each side deaf-
ened him with depreciation of the other establishment till his only conclusion was that each was
worse than the other, and that it mattered little at
which of them he paid dearly for an indigestion.
When I say that I make no distinctions between the
two parties, I must be allowed to make one exception. I mean the attempt by a portion of the Repub-
licans to utilize passions which every true lover
of his country should do his best to allay, by pro-
voking into virulence again the happily quiescent
animosities of our civil war. In saying this I do
not forget that the Democratic party was quite as
efficient in bringing that war upon us as the seced-
ing States themselves. Nor do I forget that it was
by the same sacrifice of general and permanent interests to the demands of immediate partisan advantage which is the besetting temptation of all
parties. Let bygones be bygones. Yet I may say
in passing that there was something profoundly
comic in the spectacle of a great party, with an

heroic past behind it, stating that its policy would be to prevent some unknown villains from doing something very wicked more than twenty years ago.

Parties being necessary things, it follows, of course, that there must be politicians to manage and leaders to represent and symbolize them. The desire of man to see his wishes, his prejudices, his aspirations, summed up and personified in a single representative has the permanence of an instinct. Few escape it, few are conscious of its controlling influence. The danger always is that loyalty to the man shall insensibly replace loyalty to the thing he is supposed to represent, till at last the question *what* he represents fades wholly out of mind. The love of victory as a good in itself is also a powerful ingredient in the temperament of most men. Forty odd years ago it would have been hard to find a man, no matter how wicked he may have believed the Mexican War to be, who could suppress a feeling of elation when the news of Buena Vista arrived. Never mind the principle involved, it was our side that won.

If the dangers and temptations of parties be such as I have indicated, and I do not think that I have overstated them, it is for the interest of the best men in both parties that there should be a neutral body, not large enough to form a party by itself, nay, which would lose its power for good if it attempted to form such a party, and yet large enough to moderate between both, and to make both more cautious in their choice of candidates and in their connivance with evil practices. If the politicians must look after the parties, there should be somebody to look after the politicians, somebody to ask disagreeable questions and to utter uncomfortable truths; somebody to make sure, if possible, before election, not only what, but whom the candidate, if elected, is going to represent. What to me is the saddest feature of our present methods is the pitfalls which they dig in the path of ambitious and able men who feel that they are fitted for a political career, that by character and training they could be of service to their country, yet who find every avenue closed to them unless at the sacrifice of the very independence which gives them a claim to what they seek. As in semi-barbarous times the sincerity of a converted Jew was tested by forcing him to swallow pork, so these are required to gulp without a wry face what is as nauseous to them. I would do all in my power to render such loathsome compliances unnecessary. The pity of it is that with our political methods the hand is of necessity subdued to what it works in. It has been proved, I think, that the old parties are not to be reformed from within. It is from without that the attempt must be made, and it is the Independents who must make it. If the attempt should fail, the failure of the experiment of democracy would inevitably follow.

But I do not believe that it will fail. The signs are all favorable. Already there are journals in every part of the country — journals, too, among the first in ability, circulation, and influence —

which refuse to wear the colors of party. Already the people have a chance of hearing the truth, and I think that they always gladly hear it. Our first aim should be, as it has been, the reform of our civil service, for that is the fruitful mother of all our ills. It is the most aristocratic system in the world, for it depends on personal favor and is the reward of personal service, and the power of the political boss is built up and maintained, like that of the mediæval robber baron, by his freehandedness in distributing the property of other people. From it is derived the notion that the public treasure is a fund to a share of which every one is entitled who by fraud or favor can get it, and from this again the absurd doctrine of rotation in office so that each may secure his proportion, and that the business of the nation may be carried on by a succession of apprentices who are dismissed just as they are getting an inkling of their trade to make room for others who are in due time to be turned loose on the world, passed masters in nothing but incompetence for any useful career. From this, too, has sprung the theory of the geographical allotment of patronage, as if ability were dependent, like wheat, upon the soil, and the more mischievous one that members of Congress must be residents of the district that elects them, a custom which has sometimes excluded men of proved ability, in the full vigor of their faculties and the ripeness of their experience, from the councils of the nation. All reforms seem slow and wearisome to their advocates, for these are commonly of that

ardent and imaginative temper which inaccurately
foreshortens the distance and overlooks the difficulties between means and end. If we have not got
all that we hoped from the present administration,
we have perhaps got more than we had reason to
expect, considering how widely spread are the roots
of this evil, and what an inconvenient habit they
have of sending up suckers in the most unexpected places. To cut off these does not extirpate,
them. It is the parent tree that must go. It is
much that we have compelled a discussion of the
question from one end of the country to the other,
for it cannot bear discussion, and I for one have
so much faith in the good sense of the American
people as to feel sure that discussion means victory. That the Independents are so heartily de-
nounced by those who support and are supported
by the system that has been gradually perfected
during the last fifty years is an excellent symp-
tom. We must not be impatient. Some of us
can remember when those who are now the can-
onized saints of the party which restored the
Union and abolished slavery were a forlorn hope
of Mugwumps, the scorn of all practical politicians. Sydney Smith was fond of saying that the
secret of happiness in life was to take short views,
and in this he was but repeating the rule of the
Greek and Roman poets, to live in every hour as
if we were never to have another. But he who
would be happy as a reformer must take long views,
and into distances sometimes that baffle the most
piercing vision.

Two great questions have been opened anew by the President: reduction of revenue, and the best means of effecting it, and these really resolve themselves into one, that of the war tariff. I say of the war tariff, because it is a mere electioneering device to call it a question of protection or free trade pure and simple. I shall barely allude to them as briefly as possible, for they will be amply discussed before the people by more competent men than I. I cannot help thinking that both are illustrations of the truth that it is a duty of statesmen to study tendencies and probable consequences much rather than figures, which can as easily be induced to fight impartially on both sides as the *condottieri* of four centuries ago. All that reasonable men contend for now is the reduction of the tariff in such a way as shall be least hurtful to existing interests, most helpful to the consumer, and, above all, as shall practically test the question whether we are better off when we get our raw material at the lowest possible prices. I think the advocates of protection have been unwise, and are beginning to see that they were unwise in shifting the ground of debate. They have set many people to asking whether robbing Peter to pay Paul be a method equally economical for both parties, and whether the bad policy of it be not all the more flagrant in proportion as the Peters are many and the Pauls few? Whether the Pauls of every variety be not inevitably forced into an alliance offensive and defensive against the Peters, and sometimes with very questionable people?

Whether if we are taxed for the payment of a bounty to the owner of a silver mine, we should not be equally taxed to make a present to the owner of wheat fields, cotton fields, tobacco fields, hay fields, which are the most productive gold mines of the country? Whether the case of protection be not like that of armored ships, requiring ever thicker plating as the artillery of competition is perfected? But the tendency of excessive protection which thoughtful men dread most is that it stimulates an unhealthy home competition, leading to over-production and to the disasters which are its tainted offspring; that it fosters over-population, and this of the most helpless class when thrown out of employment; that it engenders smuggling, false invoices, and other demoralizing practices; that the principle which is its root is the root also of Rings, and Syndicates, and Trusts, and all other such conspiracies for the artificial raising of profits in the interest of classes and minorities. I confess I cannot take a cheerful view of the future of that New England I love so well when her leading industries shall be gradually drawn to the South, as they infallibly will be, by the greater cheapness of labor there. It is not pleasant to hear that called the American system which has succeeded in abolishing our commercial marine. It is even less pleasant to hear it advocated as being for the interest of the laborer by men who imported cheaper labor till it was forbidden by law. The true American system is that which produces the best *men* by leaving them as much as possible to their own resources.

That protection has been the cause of our material prosperity is refuted by the passage I have already quoted from Burke. Though written when our farmers' wives and daughters did most of our spinning and weaving, one would take it for a choice flower of protection eloquence. We have prospered in spite of artificial obstacles that would have baffled a people less energetic and less pliant to opportunity. The so-called American system, the system, that is, of selfish exclusion and monopoly, is no invention of ours, but has been borrowed of the mediæval guilds. It has had nothing to do with the raising of wages, for these are always higher in countries where the demand for labor is greater than the supply. And if the measure of wages be their purchasing power, what does the workman gain, unless it be the pleasure of spending more money, under a system, which, if it pay more money in the hire of hands, enhances the prices of what that money will buy in more than equal proportion?

Of the surplus in the Treasury I will only say that it has already shown itself to be an invitation to every possible variety of wasteful expenditure and therefore of demoralizing jobbery, and that it has again revived those theories of grandmotherly government which led to our revolt from the mother country, are most hostile to the genius of our institutions, and soonest sap the energy and corrode the morals of a people.

It is through its politics, through its capacity for government, the noblest of all sciences, that a nation proves its right to a place among the other beneficent forces of nature. For politics permeate more widely than any other force, and reach every one of us, soon or late, to teach or to debauch. We are confronted with new problems and new conditions. We and the population which is to solve them are very unlike that of fifty years ago. As I was walking not long ago in the Boston Public Garden, I saw two Irishmen looking at Ball's equestrian statue of Washington, and wondering who was the personage thus commemorated. I had been brought up among the still living traditions of Lexington, Concord, Bunker's Hill, and the siege of Boston. To these men Ireland was still their country, and America a place to get their daily bread. This put me upon thinking. What, then, is patriotism, and what its true value to a man? Was it merely an unreasoning and almost cat-like attachment to certain square miles of the earth's surface, made up in almost equal parts of lifelong association, hereditary tradition, and parochial prejudice? This is the narrowest and most provincial form, as it is also, perhaps, the strongest, of that passion or virtue, whichever we choose to call it. But did it not fulfil the essential condition of giving men an ideal outside themselves, which would awaken in them capacities for devotion and heroism that are deaf even to the penetrating cry of self? All the moral good of which patriotism is the fruitful mother, my two Irishmen had in abundant measure, and it had wrought in them marvels of fidelity and self-sacrifice which made me blush for the easier terms on which my own duties of the like kind were habitually fulfilled. Were they not daily pinching themselves that they might pay their tribute to the old hearthstone or the old cause three thousand miles away? If tears tingle our eyes when we read of the like loyalty in the clansmen of the attainted and exiled Lochiel, shall this leave us unmoved?

I laid the lesson to heart. I would, in my own way, be as faithful as they to what I believed to be the best interests of my country. Our politicians are so busy studying the local eddies of prejudice or interest that they allow the main channel of our national energies to be obstructed by dams for the grinding of private grist. Our leaders no longer lead, but are as skilful as Indians in following the faintest trail of public opinion. I find it generally admitted that our moral standard in politics has been lowered, and is every day going lower. Some attribute this to our want of a leisure class. It is to a book of the Apocrypha that we are indebted for the invention of the Man of Leisure.[1] But a leisure class without a definite object in life, and without generous aims, is a bane rather than a blessing. It would end in the weariness and cynical pessimism in which its great exemplar Ecclesiastes ended, without leaving us the gift which his genius left. What we want is an active class who will insist in season and out of season that we shall

[1] " The wisdom of a learned man cometh by opportunity of leisure, and he that hath little business shall become wise." — *Ecclesiasticus* xxxviii. 24.

have a country whose greatness is measured, not only by its square miles, its number of yards woven, of hogs packed, of bushels of wheat raised, not only by its skill to feed and clothe the body, but also by its power to feed and clothe the soul; a country which shall be as great morally as it is materially; a country whose very name shall not only, as now it does, stir us as with the sound ot a trumpet, but shall call out all that is best within us by offering us the radiant image of something better and nobler and more enduring than we, of something that shall fulfil our own thwarted aspiration, when we are but a handful of forgotten dust in the soil trodden by a race whom we shall have helped to make more worthy of their inheritance than we ourselves had the power, I might almost say the means, to be.

"OUR LITERATURE"

RESPONSE TO A TOAST AT THE BANQUET IN NEW YORK, APRIL 30, 1889, GIVEN IN COMMEMORATION OF THE HUNDREDTH ANNIVERSARY OF WASHINGTON'S INAUGURATION.

A NEEDFUL frugality, benignant alike to both the participants in human utterance, has limited the allowance of each speaker this evening to ten minutes. Cut in thicker slices, our little loaf of time would not suffice for all. This seems a meagre ration, but if we give to our life the Psalmist's measure of seventy years, and bear in mind the population of the globe, a little ciphering will show that no single man and brother is entitled even to so large a share of our attention as this. Moreover, how few are the men in any generation who could not deliver the message with which their good or evil genius has charged them in less than the sixth part of an hour.

On an occasion like this, a speaker lies more than usually open to the temptation of seeking the acceptable rather than the judicial word. And yet it is inevitable that public anniversaries, like those of private persons, should suggest self-criticism as well as self-satisfaction. I shall not listen for such suggestions, though I may not altogether conceal

that I am conscious of them. I am to speak for
literature, and of our own as forming now a recognized part of it. This is not the place for critical
balancing of what we have done or left undone in
this field. An exaggerated estimate and, that indis-
criminateness of praise which implies a fear to speak
the truth, would be unworthy of myself or of you.
I might indeed read over a list of names now, alas,
carven on headstones, since it would be invidious
to speak of the living. But the list would be short,
and I could call few of the names great as the
impartial years measure greatness. I shall prefer
to assume that American literature was not worth
speaking for at all if it were not quite able to
speak for itself, as all others are expected to do.

I think this a commemoration in which it is
peculiarly fitting that literature should take part.
For we are celebrating to-day our true birthday as
a nation, the day when our consciousness of wider
interests and larger possibilities began. All that
went before was birth-throes. The day also recalls
us to a sense of something to which we are too indifferent. I mean that historic continuity, which,
as a factor in moulding national individuality, is
not only powerful in itself, but cumulative in its
operation. In one of these literature finds the soil,
and in the other the climate, it needs. Without
the stimulus of a national consciousness, no literature could have come into being; under the conditions in which we then were, none that was not
parasitic and dependent. Without the continuity
which slowly incorporates that consciousness in the

general life and thought, no literature could have acquired strength to detach itself and begin a life of its own.   And here another thought suggested by the day comes to my mind.   Since that precious and persuasive quality, style, may be exemplified as truly in a life as in a work of art, may not the character of the great man whose memory decorates this and all our days, in its dignity, its strength, its calm of passion restrained, its inviolable reserves, furnish a lesson which our literature may study to great advantage?   And not our literature alone.

Scarcely had we become a nation when the only part of the Old World whose language we understood began to ask in various tones of despondency where was our literature.   We could not improvise Virgils or Miltons, though we made an obliging effort to do it.   Failing in this, we thought the question partly unfair and wholly disagreeable. And indeed it had never been put to several nations far older than we, and to which a *vates sacer* had been longer wanting.   But, perhaps it was not altogether so ill-natured as it seemed, for, after all, a nation without a literature is imperfectly represented in the parliament of mankind.   It implied, therefore, in our case the obligation of an illustrious blood.

With a language in compass and variety inferior to none that has ever been the instrument of human thought or passion or sentiment, we had inherited also the forms and precedents of a literature altogether worthy of it.   But these forms and

precedents we were to adapt suddenly to novel
conditions, themselves still in solution, tentative,
formless, atom groping after atom, rather through
blind instinct than with conscious purpose. Why
wonder if our task proved as long as it was difficult? And it was all the more difficult that we
were tempted to free ourselves from the form as
well as from the spirit. And we had other notable
hindrances. Our reading class was small, scattered
thinly along the seaboard, and its wants were fully
supplied from abroad, either by importation or
piracy. Communication was tedious and costly.
Our men of letters, or rather our men with a natural impulsion to a life of letters, were few and
isolated, and I cannot recollect that isolation has
produced anything in literature better than monk-
ish chronicles, except a Latin hymn or two, and
one precious book, the treasure of bruised spirits.
Criticism there was none, and what assumed its
function was half provincial self-conceit, half patri-
otic resolve to find swans in birds of quite another
species. Above all, we had no capital toward which
all the streams of moral and intellectual energy
might converge to fill a reservoir on which all
could draw. There were many careers open to
ambition, all of them more tempting and more
gainful than the making of books. Our people
were of necessity largely intent on material ends,
and our accessions from Europe tended to increase
this predisposition. Considering all these things, it
is a wonder that in these hundred years we should
have produced any literature at all; a still greater

wonder that we have produced so much of which we may be honestly proud. Its English descent is and must always be manifest, but it is ever more and more informed with a new spirit, more and more trustful in the guidance of its own thought. But if we would have it become all that we would have it be, we must beware of judging it by a comparison with its own unripe self alone. We must not cuddle it into weakness or wilfulness by over-indulgence. It would be more profitable to think that we have as yet no literature in the highest sense than to insist that what we have should be judged by other than admitted standards, merely because it is ours. In these art matches we must not only expect but rejoice to be pitted against the doughtiest wrestlers, and the lightest-footed runners of all countries and of all times.

Literature has been put somewhat low on the list of toasts, doubtless in deference to necessity of arrangement, but perhaps the place assigned to it here may be taken as roughly indicating that which it occupies in the general estimation. And yet I venture to claim for it an influence, whether for good or evil, more durable and more widely operative than that exerted by any other form in which human genius has found expression. As the special distinction of man is speech, it should seem that there can be no higher achievement of civilized men, no proof more conclusive that they are civilized men, than the power of moulding words into such fair and noble forms as shall people the human mind forever with images that refine, console, and inspire. It is no vain superstition that has made the name of Homer sacred to all who love a bewitchingly simple and yet ideal picture of our human life in its doing and its suffering. And there are books which have kept alive and transmitted the spark of soul that has resuscitated nations. It is an old wives' tale that Virgil was a great magician, yet in that tale survives a witness of the influence which made him, through Dante, a main factor in the revival of Italy after the one had been eighteen and the other five centuries in their graves.

I am not insensible to the wonder and exhilaration of a material growth without example in rapidity and expansion, but I am also not insensible to the grave perils latent in any civilization which allows its chief energies and interests to be wholly absorbed in the pursuit of a mundane prosperity. "Rejoice, O young man, in thy youth; and let thy heart cheer thee in the days of thy youth: but know thou, that for all these things God will bring thee into judgment."

I admire our energy, our enterprise, our inventiveness, our multiplicity of resource, no man more; but it is by less visibly remunerative virtues, I persist in thinking, that nations chiefly live and feel the higher meaning of their lives. Prosperous we may be in other ways, contented with more specious successes, but that nation is a mere horde supplying figures to the census which does not acknowledge a truer prosperity and a richer contentment in the things of the mind. Railways and

telegraphs reckoned by the thousand miles are excellent things in their way, but I doubt whether it
be of their poles and sleepers that the rounds are
made of that ladder by which men or nations scale
the cliffs whose inspiring obstacle interposes itself
between them and the fulfilment of their highest
purpose and function.

The literature of a people should be the record
of its joys and sorrows, its aspirations and its shortcomings, its wisdom and its folly, the confidant of
its soul. We cannot say that our own as yet suffices us, but I believe that he who stands, a hundred
years hence, where I am standing now, conscious
that he speaks to the most powerful and prosperous community ever devised or developed by man,
will speak of our literature with the assurance of
one who beholds what we hope for and aspire
after, become a reality and a possession forever.

GENERAL INDEX

A. H. C. = A. H. Clough.

Abana and Pharpar, 1, 364.

Abbott, *Shakespearian grammar*, 4, 108 n.

Abderite chorus in the *Andromeda*, 1, 92.

Abelard, Emerson before the Φ. B. K. compared to, 1, 367.

Abolition societies existed in Maryland and Virginia in 1790, 5, 141.

Abolitionists not the cause of the war, 5, 203; their cardinal principle disunion, 204; *also*, 6, 201.

Abstract ideas, Hazlitt on, 4, 85.

Abundance of Chaucer and Langland, 3, 331.

Abuse unpleasant from inferiors, 1, 226.

Abuses to be protested against, 5, 14.

Academic town. *See* University town.

Accent in Milton's verse, 4, 109, 112.

Accidente, Italian imprecation, 1, 172.

Accuracy and Truth compared, 6, 153.

Acephali, 1, 111.

Achilles, chariot of, 1, 152; a boy with an eel compared to, 217; *also*, 2, 5.

Acting, Italian, 1, 175. *See also*, Stage.

Adam in Paradise, White's Selborne the Journal of, 3, 193.

Adams, Charles Francis, on the attitude of America toward England in 1869, 3, 253.

Adams, John, J. Quincy's reminiscences of, 2, 295.

Adams, *Parson. See* Fielding, Henry.

Addison, friendship with Dryden, 3, 104; Pope's attack on, 178; answers an argument in favor of the Pretender, 4, 26; Pope's lines on, 45; Pope's relations to, 52; his character, 53; *also*, 3, 357, 363.

on Italy, 1, 127; on English poetry of the 18th century, 4, 3; on the representation of common sense, the office of modern writers, 46.

Cato, Voltaire on, 4, 17.

Adhesiveness, the author's, 1, 51.

Adrian V., Pope, in the *Divine Comedy*, 4, 240.

Æschylus, his range narrow but deep, 1, 365; 4, 261; Atalanta in Corydon the theme of a lost drama, 2, 126; like Shakespeare in his choice of epithets, 3, 51; his imaginative power, 6, 52; *also*, 2, 138, 286; 3, 45, 301.

Agamemnon, the nurse, 3, 54; *Prometheus*, 39, 57; *Seven against Thebes*, passage cited, 54.

Æsthetic defects, connection with moral defects, 2, 91.

Æsthetics, Shakespeare's satire on the dogmatic variety, 3, 55; its problems recur in Wordsworth's poetry, 4, 357.

Affliction a cooler of pride, Roger Williams on, 2, 29.

Africa, a little mystery still hangs over the interior of, 1, 109.

Agamemnon, 1, 263.

Agassiz, Louis, anecdote of his first lecture; 6, 9; *also*, 3, 240, 286; 6, 149.

Age, the respect for, diminishing, 6, 137. *See also*, Old age; Antiquity.

Agrippa, Cornelius, on Dante, 4, 145; his visionary gardens, 397.

Ague, Sir K. Digby's prescription for, 2, 56.

Air, on a winter morning, 3, 283.

Ajax, 2, 172; 3, 85.

Akenside on winter, 3, 266; his poetry characterized, 266; Spenser's influence upon, 4, 352; *also*, 6, 113. his *Pleasures of Imagination*, 2, 143; 4, 3.

Alabama trouble, the relations between England and America caused by, 3, 252.

Alban mountain, 1, 139; seen from Palestrina, 159.

Albani, Villa, near Rome, 1, 214.

Alberti, Leandro, on Italy, 1, 126.

Alchemist visited by Edw. Howes, 2, 46; Coleridge compared to, 6, 70.

Gilchrist, his controversy with Bowles, **4**, 54.

Gill, Alexander, **4**, 123.

Giotto, **4**, 119; Dante his friend, 125.

Giraldi, **3**, 364.

Glacier, encroachments of slavery compared to, **5**, 43.

Gladiators, **5**, 126.

Gladstone, W. E., **6**, 208.

Glanvil, Joseph, accounts of witchcraft, **2**, 338; on the alleged transportation of witches, 354; believed in witchcraft, 377; his *Sadducismus Triumphatus*, 11.

Glass model of a ship in the Cambridge barber's shop, **1**, 63.

Glaucus, **2**, 79.

Glees, **4**, 97.

Gleim, Joh. Wilh. Lud., **2**, 197, 200; Lessing's advice to, 203.

Gliddon, **5**, 220.

Glory, departed, its ghost lingers, **1**, 191. *See also*, Fame.

God, the Emperor of Heaven in Dante's idea, **4**, 242 n; Dante's vision of, 256; the methods of the divine justice, **5**, 123. *See also*, Providence.

Godeau, on snow, **3**, 275.

Goethe, Carlyle and Emerson both disciples of, **1**, 367; attracted to alchemy, **2**, 47; the imaginative quality in his works uniform, 85; his influence on Carlyle, 85; a European poet, 121; Schiller's verses to, quoted, 124; his comedies dull, 146; his struggle to emancipate himself from Germany, 150; lack of coherence in his longer works, 167; early notes to Frau von Stein, 168; in *Werthermontirung*, 169; grandness of his figure, 172; sacrificed morality to poetic sense, 195; his visit to Gottsched, 218; takes pleasure in his hypothetical despair, 251; essentially an observer, and incapable of partisanship, **3**, 2; got his knowledge of classics second hand, 46; uncontemporaneous nature, 101; paid slight attention to Dante, **4**, 145; early love of Gothic, 235; possibly influenced Wordsworth, 380; compared with Wordsworth, 413; his teaching of self-culture, **6**, 103; *also*, **1**, 357 364; **2**, 174, 187, 207 n, 308; **3**, 25, 301, 355; **4**, 61, 161.

on the failure to escape one's own shadow, **1**, 121; on Italy, 126; on the German idea of humor, **2**, 90; on the office of the Muse, 108; on Milton's *Samson Agonistes*, 133; on Le sing as a genius, 231; on the distinction between the ancient and modern drama, **3**, 57; on Shakespeare, 63, 66; on Hamlet, 87; compares a poem to a painted window, 67; on destructive and productive

criticism, 67; on **thinking pen** in **hand**, 123; on the French drama, 162; on snow in sunshine, 267.

Achilleis, **2**, 129; **3**, 47; *Faust*, written without thought of its deeper meaning, 90; the second part, **2**, 139, 168; **4**, 145; *Götz von Berlichingen*, **3**, 63; — *Harz-reise im Winter*, 267; — *Hermann und Dorothea*, **2**, 129; **3**, 46; — *Iphigenie*, **2**, 133; — *Roman Idylls*, 129; — *Ueber allen Gipfeln*, **4**, 370; — *Werther*, **2**, 251; — *Wilhelm Meister*, 167; Wordsworth on, **4**, 380.

Götz of the Iron Hand, Carlyle's type of the highest, **2**, 94.

Goffe, Col., of Deerfield, **2**, 292; Prof. P. compared to, **1**, 93.

Gold of the poet, **2**, 78.

Golden age, behind every generation, **2**, 98.

Gold-fish in a vase compared to self-absorbed travellers, **1**, 49.

Goldsmith, his description of a mutual admiration society, **2**, 201; his figure of the 'lengthening chain,' **3**, 136 n; Wordsworth familiar with, **4**, 360 n, 361; his influence on Wordsworth, 369, 370; *also*, **3**, 357, 364.

Deserted Village, **2**, 135; **4**, 370; — *Traveller*, 370; — *Vicar of Wakefield*, **2**, 104, 168.

Golias, Bishop, **1**, 84; **6**, 151; his motto appropriate for Americans, **1**, 199.

Gongora, poet of the cultist school, **4**, 8.

Gonzales, Manuel, on servants in London, **2**, 45.

Good, in itself infinitely and eternally lovely, **5**, 130; its conquests silent and beneficent, 176.

Good luck, **4**, 391.

Good nature, **6**, 42; Dryden on, **3**, 176; fostered by a democracy, **6**, 97.

Good society, **3**, 232; Dante's notions of, **4**, 176; to be found more easily in books than in the world, **6**, 84.

Good taste the conscience of the mind, **6**, 178.

Goodliness of the world, **3**, 222.

Goose, Mother. *See* Mother Goose, **3**, 338.

Gorboduc. See Sackville.

Gosling, Lady, her obituary, **2**, 219.

Gothic, lack of agreement with the Roman, **1**, 193.

Gothic cathedral, impressiveness and nobleness of, **1**, 206; unmatched in ancient art, 212; the visible symbol of an inward faith, **4**, 234; compared to the *Divine Comedy*, 236.

Gottsched, Lessing on, **2**, 175; his *Art of poetry*, 218; Goethe's visit to,

Heathen, Dante on their state after death, **4**, 248.

Heathen divinities. *See* Pagan divinities.

Heather, its American substitute, **1**, 13.

Hebrew literature, **4**, 234.

Hector, **2**, 104, 296.

Hecuba, **2**, 21.

Heeren, Bancroft's translation of, **6**, 157.

Heidegger, Dr., **2**, 300.

Heine, his airy humor, **2**, 90; his style, 167; his want of inward propriety, 170; his cynicism, 229; turned the Gods of Greece to good account, 327; on the nature of woman, 358; his profound pathos, **6**, 56; influenced by Spanish romances, 116; the first English translation of, 157; hated the Romans for inventing Latin grammar, 164; *also*, **1**, 364; **3**, 259, 301.

Helen of Kirconnel, Wordsworth's version compared with the original, **4**, 403 n.

Helen of Troy, **1**, 32.

Helias, St., **2**, 368 n.

Hell, imagined as the reverse of Heaven, **2**, 349; Dante's picture of, **4**, 175; Marlowe on, 175.

Hemingе and Condell, **3**, 20.

Henchmen, **1**, 176.

Henry IV. of France at Ivry, a Roman policeman compared to, **1**, 216; compared with Lincoln in character and circumstances, **5**, 190.

Henry VII., Emperor, his expedition to Italy, **4**, 133; his death, 134.

Henry IX. of England, so-called, **2**, 274.

Hens. *See* Fowls.

Heraclitus, **1**, 165.

Herakles and Simson, **2**, 134.

Herbert, George, character of his poems, **1**, 254; *also*, **4**, 21 n; quoted, **6**, 165.

Herbert of Cherbury, Lord, on riding, **4**, 351.

Herder, **2**, 169, 219; his love-letters, 208.

Heredity, **3**, 315; influence of, in great men, **4**, 362; makes all men in a sense coeval, **6**, 138. *See also*, Ancestry.

Heresy, Selden on, **2**, 216; Dante had no sympathy with, **4**, 244.

Heretics, Lessing on, **2**, 199; the persecution of, 374.

Hermit, who became a king, a mediæval apologue, **5**, 1.

Hermit instinct strong in New England, **1**, 89.

Hero, Carlyle's picture of, **2**, 93; a makeshift of the past, 106; eagerly accepted by a nation, **5**, 93.

Herodias in legend, **2**, 358.

Herodotus, Plutarch on, **3**, 231.

Heroic treatment demanded for trifling occasions, **5**, 198.

Heroism the touch of nature that makes the whole world kin, **6**, 42.

Herrick, Hazlitt's edition of, **1**, 320; *also*, **2**, 223; **4**, 369; — *On Julia's Petticoat*, **3**, 124.

Hertzberg, Wilh., Geoffrey Chaucer's Canterbury-Geschichten, **3**, 291, 298.

Hesperides, apples of, true poems compared to, **4**, 266.

Heylin, Dr., on French cooks, **3**, 119.

Heywood's *Four P. P.* quoted, **1**, 337; his *Woman killed with kindness* quoted on the condition of prisons in old England, 159.

Hibbins, Mr., **2**, 27.

Higginson, T. W., preacher and soldier, **2**, 286.

Highlanders. *See* Scotch Highlanders.

Hildesheim, Bishop of, his demon-cook, **2**, 366.

Hill, Aaron, Pope's correspondence with, **4**, 52.

Hippocrene, **4**, 89.

Hippolytus. *See* Euripides.

Hirschel lawsuit, Lessing employed as a translator in, **2**, 187.

Historians, Raleigh's warning to, **3**, 54; **4**, 319 n.

Historic continuity, its effect on national individuality, **6**, 223.

Historical composition, the value of anecdote and scandal in, **2**, 284; the modern fashion of picturesque writing, **4**, 64; the value of contemporary memoirs, 65; **5**, 241, 242; the so-called dignity of, often mere dulness, **4**, 66; the Johnsonian swell of the last century, 67; importance of good taste in, 67; value of personal testimony, **5**, 118; distorted by bad logic and by the style of the writer, 120; truth of circumstance combined with error in character, 121; the annalist's method, 121; the "standard" histories, 121; the poet's view of, 123; the historical romance, 123; the epic style, 123; the partisan method, 124; the forlorn-hope method, 124; the *a priori* fashion, 124; the ancient method, 277.

Historical insight, **2**, 111.

Historical romance, **5**, 123.

History, its key to be found in America, **1**, 53; without the soil it grew in, its shortcomings, 113; cycles in the movement of, 191; **5**, 126; its humors, **2**, 22; the hero in, 74; Carlyle's scheme of, 99; the place of popular opinion in, 99; events gain in greatness from the stage on which they occur, 275; its field generally limited, 278; made largely by igno-

language, 241 ; originality, 241 ; compared with Wordsworth and Byron, 242 ; his poetic imagination, 243 ; an example of the Renaissance, 244 ; power of assimilation, 244 ; self-denial in use of language, 244 ; power of poetic expression, 245 ; his poems a reaction against the barrel-organ style of poetry, 245 ; the greatness and purity of his poetic gift, 246 ; should have translated Homer, 289 ; learned to versify from Chapman, 296 ; denunciation of 18th century style, 3, 98 ; studied Dryden's versification, 99 n ; his style compared with Milton's, 4, 86 ; Spenser's influence upon, 352 ; *also*, 3, 326.
on the imagination, 1, 243 ; on Chapman's Homer, 4, 294 ; on continuations of an ancient story by great poets, 312 ; on a line of Shakespeare's, 409 n.
Endymion, 1, 225, 230, 244 ; 3, 354 ; — *Hyperion*, 1, 235, 244 ; — *Lamia*, 235, 244 ; — *Lyrical Ballads*, 226 ; — *Odes*, 244 ; — *Ode to a Grecian Urn*, 4, 371 n ; — *Sonnets*, 1, 244.
Kemble, John, in Macbeth, 3, 70.
Kent, men of, their tails, 1, 112.
Kepler, 3, 16.
Ketch, Jack, 3, 176.
Kidd, Capt., 5, 119.
Kineo, Maine, 1, 18.
Kineo, Mount, 1, 13 ; ascent of, 39.
Kings, Browning's picture of a king, 2, 109 ; 6, 27 ; their Sacred Majesty ridiculed by the Dutch, 3, 234.
Kirke, Edmund, probably the same as Spenser, 4, 301 n.
Kirkland, President, his character, 1, 83 ; his appearance, 84 ; unsuited to his time, 85 ; anecdotes of him, 86 ; his manner of praying, 88.
Kleist, Lessing on, 2, 173 ; Lessing's friendship with, 197.
Klopstock, 2, 219 ; Lessing on, 176 ; Wordsworth's interview with, 4, 379.
on the German Muse, 2, 183.
Klotz, Lessing's criticism of, 2, 200.
Knebel, his judgment of Frederick the Great, 2, 113.
Knight of Courtesy, Hazlitt's and Ritson's editions of, 1, 331.
Knights of Labor, 6, 183.
Knives, the Chief Mate's appreciation of, 1, 114.
Knowledge, elements of, 1, 48 ; that which comes of sympathy, 3, 49.
Knowledge and learning, 2, 186.
Know-Nothings, 5, 318.
Knox, John, 2, 265.
Kobes I., Emperor, his speeches compared to Pres. Johnson's, 5, 289.
König, Eva, Lessing's wife, 2, 207.

L. S. = Leslie Stephen.
Labor, cheap, importation of, 6, 217.
Labor-saving contrivances, 2, 279.
La Bruyère on witchcraft, 2, 387.
La Chevrette, Hermitage of, 1, 375.
La Fontaine, 2, 200.
Lager-beer and brandy, the Dutchman's distinction, 1, 127.
Laing, editor of Dunbar's works, 4, 271.
Lake, its uncanny noises on a freezing night, 3, 290.
Lamartine, 2, 236, 266, 271 ; 3, 262 ; resents the subsidy granted him by the Senate, 2, 258 ; autumn compared to, 3, 259.
Lamb, Charles, his criticism of the English dramatists, 3, 29 ; his defence of the comedy of the Restoration, 150 ; Wordsworth's friendship with, 4, 386 ; *also*, 1, 249, 251 ; 3, 280 ; 5, 133.
on Webster, 1, 280 ; on Spenser, 4, 326 ; on Wordsworth, 390.
his *Essays of Elia*, 6, 82.
Lamb, Charles and Mary, 4, 363 n.
Lamennais on Dante, 4, 163.
La Motte Fouqué. *See* Fouqué.
Lamps, alchemists', Pope's teaching in the *Essay on Man* compared to, 4, 37.
Lance-rests, 1, 328.
Land, Henry George's theories of, 6, 35.
Land companies. *See* American land companies.
Land speculations, Rufus Davenport's, in Cambridgeport, 1, 71.
Landino, comment on Dante, 4, 156.
Landor, Walter Savage, 2, 123 ; his *Gebirus Rex*, 129 ; his pseudo-classicism, 135 ; his style compared with Milton's, 4, 86 ; his blank-verse, 399.
on great men, 3, 104 ; on mingling prose with poetry, 144 ; on Spenser, 4, 352 ; on Wordsworth, 401 ; on Napoleon III., 5, 125 ; on Coleridge's criticism of *Don Quixote*, 6, 126.
Landscape, described by Chaucer, 3, 261, 357 ; value of human associations in, 6, 139. *See also*, Nature ; Scenery ; Views.
Landscape-gardeners of literature, 3, 189.
Langland, 3, 324 ; compared with Chaucer, 330 ; his verse, 332 ; charm of his language, 335.
Piers Ploughman, reprinted in the "Library of Old Authors," 1, 252 ; its language, 3, 11 ; as an example of popular poetry, 334 ; cited, 1, 326 ; 2, 328.
Language, growth of, 1, 373 ; 3, 328 ; power of, 1, 245 ; must catch its fire from the thought behind it, 2, 122 ; its purity dependent on veracity of

the associations connected with, **2**, 273 ; Milton's use of, **4**, 105 ; the limitations of, **6**, 193.

Nannucci, Intorno alle voci usate da Dante, **4**, 169 n.

Napier, **1**, 31.

Naples. *See also*, Neapolitans.

Napoleon I., his portrait in the Cambridge barber's shop, **1**, 62 ; compared with Frederick the Great, **2**, 114 ; fails to recognize Bolivar, 283 ; recipe for saving life in dealing with a mob, **5**, 84 ; at St. Helena, 97 ; the moralist's view of, 129 ; on the French Revolution, **6**, 33 ; *also*, **2**, 237 ; **5**, 23.

Napoleon III., **5**, 23, 129 ; unappreciated before the *coup d'état* of 1851, 125.

Narrative, who can write it well, **1**, 121 ; wearisome to Carlyle, **2**, 102.

Narrative poetry, **3**, 351 ; faults of, **4**, 321. *See also*, Descriptive poetry.

Narrow range of many great men, **1**, 365.

Nash on Harvey's hexameters, **4**, 278 n.

Nations, their manhood tried by dangers and opportunities, **5**, 63 ; their readiness to accept a hero, 93 ; symbolized as women, 94 ; the sins of, 128.

National character, the effect on, of postponing moral to material interests, **5**, 88.

National instinct in the Prussian people, **2**, 100.

National pride of the Old World and the New **2**, 1.

National success, the true measure of, **6**, 174.

Nationality, in poetry, **2**, 150 ; in literature, tending to disappear, 152 ; its germ in provincialism, 279 ; hampered in America, 280 ; as a quality in literature, **4**, 270 ; **6**, 115 ; the feeling lacking in America before the Civil War, **5**, 211 ; its effect on the life of man, 216.

Natural, the meaning of the word varies from one generation to another, **2**, 373.

Naturalness, **1**, 375 ; in literature, **2**, 83 ; **3**, 357. *See also*, Unconventionality.

Nature, Moore's view of, **1**, 103 ; modern sentimentalism about, 375 ; man's connection with, its most interesting aspect, 376 ; in Thoreau's writings, 381 ; her indifference to man, **2**, 131 ; as viewed by Rousseau and the sentimentalists, 266 ; the early view of, 319 ; the free shows provided by, **3**, 257 ; Chaucer's love of, 355 ; the love of, a modern thing, 260 ; ignored by French criticism, **4**, 9 ; its double

meanings, 258 ; Wordsworth on the infinite variety of, 368 ; its effect on the imaginative and the solitary, **6**, 104 ; descriptions of, as employed by the great poets, 111. *See also*, Landscape ; Scenery ; Views.

Nature of things, the difficulty of discovering and of accommodating our lives to, **6**, 120.

Nature-cure of Wordsworth and others, **4**, 411.

Navagero, Bernardo, on the classes in Austria in 1546, **6**, 14.

Neapolitans, their laziness, **1**, 131.

Neatness, a characteristic of Washington Allston, **1**, 72 ; the faculty of, bestowed by destiny on some men, 73.

Nebuchadnezzar cited as an instance of men turned into beasts, **2**, 360.

Neglect not an evidence of genius, **2**, 147.

Negro plots in New York in 1741, **2**, 375.

Negro suffrage, advocated, **5**, 228 ; insisted upon as essential, 261 ; demanded by the Radical party, 303 ; not to be expected from the South itself, 311. *See also*, Reconstruction.

Negroes, effect of slavery upon, **5**, 224 ; prejudice against, less strong at the South, 231. *See also*, Colored soldiers ; Freedmen ; Slavery.

Nelson, his conception of his country, **6**, 104.

Neptune in a *tête-à-tête*, rather monotonous, **1**, 101.

Neptune, Planet, discovery of, **5**, 120.

Nero, Leopoldo's historical scapegoat, **1**, 142.

Netherlands, Dante's system compared to the Constitution of, **4**, 152.

NEW ENGLAND TWO CENTURIES AGO, **2**, 1-76 ; the record of its history in the life of to-day, 1 ; faith in God, in man, and in work, the spirit of its founders, 2 ; its history dry and unpicturesque seen from without, 2 ; the central idea and intention of its founders, 3 ; reaction of their principles upon England, 4 ; the humorous side of its history brought out by Irving, and the poetic by Cooper, 5 ; the charge of fanaticism unfounded, 6, 9 ; the founders builders from the beginning, not destroyers, 8 ; enthusiasts but not fanatics, 9 ; the settlement of New England a business venture, 9 ; dealings with sectaries, 10 ; the witchcraft delusion, 10 ; decline of Puritanism, 12 ; New England the outgrowth of English Puritanism, 13 ; the early establishment of common schools, 15 ; its far-reaching importance, 17 ; the

Peculiarities of character less hidden in old times, **1**, 95.

Pedagogus, St., **1**, 79.

Pedantry, of German 18th cent. literature, **2**, 220; Montaigne began the crusade against, 221; holds sacred the dead shells, 359; the dangers of, **6**, 152.

Peel, Sir Robert, gives Wordsworth a pension, **4**, 393.

Pegasus, **1**, 220; supposed advertisement for, 196.

Pelli as a critic of Dante, **4**, 164.

Pendleton, democratic candidate for Vice-President in 1864, **5**, 154.

Penitence, Dryden's lines on, **3**, 167.

Penn, William, **3**, 218.

Penobscot River, the west branch, **1**, 33.

Pentameters, rhymed, compared to thin ice, **3**, 136 n.

Pepperell, Sir William, **2**, 274.

Pepys, the only sincere diarist in English, **1**, 121; his perfect frankness and unconsciousness, **2**, 261; the value of his memoirs, 285; his *Diary*, **3**, 134 n; *also*, **1**, 250; **2**, 79.

on Dryden's *Annus Mirabilis*, **3**, 134; on the *Maiden Queen*, 135 n; on the *Wild Gallant*, 147; on *Evening Love*, 148; on the *Indian Emperor*, acted at Court, 175 n.

PERCIVAL, JAMES GATES, LIFE AND LETTERS OF, **2**, 140–161; character of his poetry, 141; comparisons, 141, 142; his failure to learn that the world did not want his poetry, 142; compared with Akenside, 143; a professor of poetry rather than a poet, 143; his faculty artificial, not innate, 144; the literary influences to which he was subjected, 144; his unappeasable dulness, 146; his lack of systematic training, 146; his complaints of neglected genius, 147, 159; the times propitious to mediocrity, 148; hailed by the critics as the great American poet, 154; found tedious by the public, 155; an example of the too numerous class of feeble poets, 158; his miscellaneous equipment for work, 159; his opportunities and failures, 160; his attempt at suicide, 160; as a geologist and linguist, 161.

his *Imprecation*, **2**, 144; *Mind*, 143; *Prometheus*, 141.

Perham, **2**, 282.

Periodical publication, the fashion encourages sensationalism, **2**, 82.

Periphrases, **1**, 295; **4**, 10.

Perkins, Mr., the painful, **2**, 13.

Persecution, Puritan attitude toward, **6**, 145.

Persigny, **2**, 276.

Personality becoming of less account, **5**, 131.

Personification, **3**, 354; **4**, 324; alphabetic, **3**, 96; the natural instinct for, **6**, 104.

Peru, **2**, 273.

Peter, St., his miracles in Rome, **1**, 154; Southwell's version of his "Complaint," 253.

Peter of Abano, one of the earliest unbelievers in witchcraft, **2**, 381.

Peter, Hugh, life and execution, **2**, 24; his character, 25; his relations to Mrs. Sheffield, 25; Endicott's comment on, 27; his coquetting with Mrs. Ruth, 27; later notices of, 28; letter desiring an Indian servant, 43.

Petrarch, a sentimentalist, **1**, 100, 376; **2**, 253; his understanding with Death, 254; his moral inconsistency, 255; his sonnets compared with Michel Angelo's, 256; his influence on modern literature, 256; his genuine qualities, 256; probability of Chaucer's meeting with, **3**, 294; his exquisite artifice, 303; Byron on his excellence in execution, **4**, 42; *also*, **2**, 105, 155; **3**, 260; **4**, 160.

Africa, **2**, 129; *Laura*, **4**, 349.

Pettigrew, Colonel, **5**, 59.

Peucerus, Gaspar, on lycanthropy, **2**, 362.

Pheidias, **3**, 38 n.

Phi Beta Kappa Society, Emerson's oration before, **1**, 366.

Philadelphia convention of 1866, compared to the Irishman's kettle of soup, **5**, 283; compared to a circus, 285; its problem to make a patent reconciliation cement from fire and gunpowder, 286; compared to a ship stuck in a mud-bank, 287; the Resolutions and Address, 287; its real principle the power of the President, 288; its constituents, 288; attitude toward reconstruction, 301; the measures advocated, 318.

Philip, St., cited as a case of corporeal deportation, **2**, 353.

Philip II., the ambassador's answer to, **2**, 108.

Philips, Ambrose, description of ice-coated trees, **3**, 280; his love for nature, 280.

Philisterei, the revolt against, **1**, 363.

Philistines, **3**, 189.

Phillips, Edward, his *Theatrum Poetarum* reflects Milton's judgments, **4**, 1; on true poetry, 2; on the use of rhyme, 22.

Phillips, Wendell, of kin to Josiah Quincy, **2**, 297.

Phillips Andover Academy, J. Quincy at, **2**, 297.

Philosophical poetry, **6**, 112.

www.ingramcontent.com/pod-product-compliance
Lightning Source LLC
Chambersburg PA
CBHW020952030726
47496CB00005B/1466